Kingfisher
Science
Encyclopedia

General Editor: Catherine Headlam

4

FARADAY, MICHAEL ● HERBICIDE

Kingfisher

KINGFISHER
an imprint of Larousse plc
Elsley House, 24–30 Great Titchfield Street
London W1P 7AD

First published by Kingfisher 1991
Reprinted 1993, 1995 (with revisions) (twice), 1997

British Library Cataloguing-in-Publication Data
A catalogue record for this book is available from the British Library

ISBN 1 85697 450 2

Typesetting: Tradespools Ltd, Frome,
Somerset
Printed in Spain

GENERAL EDITOR
Catherine Headlam

EDITORIAL DIRECTOR
Jim Miles

ASSISTANT EDITORS
Lee Simmons
Charlotte Evans

EDITORIAL ASSISTANT
Andrea Moran

CONSULTANTS
Professor Lawrence F. Lowery, University of California, Berkeley, USA
Alison Porter, Education Officer, Science Museum, London

EDUCATIONAL CONSULTANTS
Terry Cash, Coordinator of a team of advisory teachers in Essex
Robert Pressling, Maths Coordinator,
Hillsgrove Primary School, London

CONTRIBUTORS
Joan Angelbeck
Michael Chinery
John Clark
Neil Curtis
Gwen Edmonds
Andrew Fisher
William Gould
Ian Graham
William Hemsley
James Muirden
John Paton
Brian Ward
Wendy Wasels
Peter Way

DESIGN
Ralph Pitchford
Allan Hardcastle
Ross George
Judy Crammond

PICTURE RESEARCH
Tim Russell
Elaine Willis

PRODUCTION
Dawn Hickman

SAFETY CODE

Some science experiments can be dangerous. Ask an adult to help you with difficult hammering or cutting and any experiments that involve flames, hot liquids or chemicals. Do not forget to put out any flames and turn off the heat when you have finished. Good scientists avoid accidents.

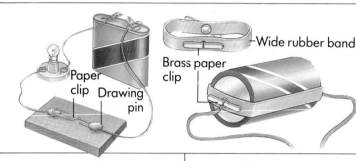

Paper clip
Drawing pin
Wide rubber band
Brass paper clip

ELECTRICITY
• Never use mains electricity for experiments.
• Use batteries for all experiments that need electricity. Dispose of batteries carefully when they are used up and never heat them up or take them apart.

HEATING
• Tie back hair and be careful of loose clothes.
• Only heat small quantities of a substance.
• Always have an adult with you.
• Never heat any container with a top on it. Always point what you are heating away from you.
• Never hold something in your hands to heat it. Use a holder that does not conduct heat.

SAFE SOURCES OF HEAT
• Hot water from the tap or kettle is a good source of heat.
• A hair dryer can be used to dry things. Always take care when using electricity near water.

• For direct heat use a night light or short thick candle placed in sand in a metal tray.

Sand
Metal tray

CHEMICALS AND QUANTITIES
• Only use a small amount of any substance even if it is just salt or vinegar.
• Never taste or eat chemicals
• Clean up all spillages immediately, especially if on your skin.
• Wash your hands after using chemicals.
• Always ask an adult before using any substance; many cooking or cleaning substances used at home are quite powerful.
• Smell chemicals very carefully. Do not breathe in deeply any strong smells.
• Never handle chemicals with your bare hands. Use an old spoon and wash it very carefully after use.
• Label **all** chemicals.

SUN
• Never look directly at the Sun, especially when using a telescope or binoculars.

PLANTS AND ANIMALS
• Never pick wild flowers.
• Collect insects carefully so as not to harm them. Release them afterwards.
• Be careful of stinging insects.

SAFE CONTAINERS
• Use plastic containers if an experiment does not require heating or strong chemicals.
• Use heat-proof glass or metal containers if you are using heat.
• Avoid using ordinary glass as it may shatter.

CUTTING
• Use scissors rather than a knife whenever possible.
• When using a knife keep your fingers behind the cutting edge.
• Put what you are cutting on a board that will not slip and will prevent damage to the surface underneath.

Faraday, Michael

Michael Faraday (1791–1867) was a British physicist and chemist. His experiments are the basis for our understanding of the forces of ELECTRICITY and MAGNETISM. His father was a blacksmith and Faraday had very little formal education, but he read science books in the shop where he worked. He went to Humphry DAVY's lectures at the Royal Institution in London and persuaded Davy to let him work as his assistant. In 1821, he began to study the magnetic effects of an electric current which Oersted had discovered. He became the director of the Royal Institution in 1825 and in 1831 he found that when he moved a magnet through a coil of wire, an electric current was produced in the wire. This enabled him to make the first electrical GENERATOR or dynamo. He also investigated ELECTROLYSIS.

▲ *Faraday invented the dynamo and discovered elements by using electrolysis.*

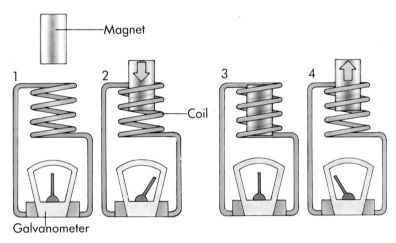

Galvanometer

◀ *In one of his experiments Faraday used a galvanometer, a device that detects electric current, to investigate the flow of current. He showed that current flows in a wire only if a magnet is put into or taken out of the coil 2 and 4. When the magnet is stationary outside or inside the coil, no current flows 1 and 3.*

▼ *About three-quarters of the world's production of fats and oils comes from vegetable oils.*

Fats

A fat is one of a group of complex organic COMPOUNDS (consisting of carbon, hydrogen and oxygen) existing in both animals and plants. A fat is an important, highly concentrated source of ENERGY for animals and plants. It provides an insulating layer under the SKIN to keep HEAT from escaping from an animal's body. It also forms the outer membrane of CELLS.

Fats can be solid and hard at room temperature, such as beef fat; solid and soft, such as butter, lard or MARGARINE; or liquid, such as vegetable oil. Liquid fats are known as OILS. Fats belong to a class of natural compounds called *lipids*, which also includes waxes. Fats are insoluble in water but will dissolve in certain ALCOHOLS.

Sources of oils and fats

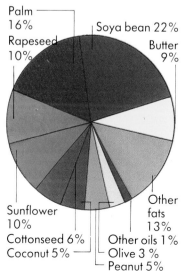

Palm 16%
Rapeseed 10%
Soya bean 22%
Butter 9%
Sunflower 10%
Cottonseed 6%
Coconut 5%
Other oils 1%
Olive 3%
Peanut 5%
Other fats 13%

▶ Cooking oil is made largely from vegetable oils but animal fats are also used. Products such as chemicals, soap and candles can be made from cow's milk and palm oil. Whales were a popular source of fat for hundreds of years but they are now protected and whales can only be caught for scientific purposes.

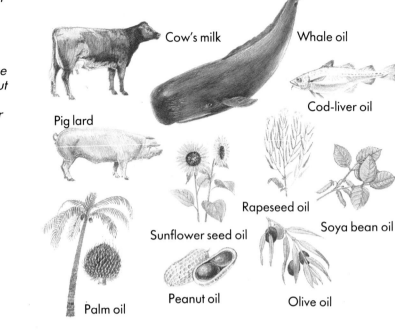

Cow's milk

Whale oil

Cod-liver oil

Pig lard

Rapeseed oil

Soya bean oil

Sunflower seed oil

Palm oil

Peanut oil

Olive oil

▼ Fat molecules consist of three fatty acid chains joined to a molecule of glycerol. Saturated fats have chains in which the carbon atoms are linked to as many hydrogen atoms as possible. In unsaturated fat chains fewer hydrogen atoms are linked to the carbon atoms, resulting in a double bond.

Saturated fat

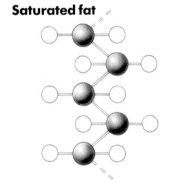

Unsaturated fat

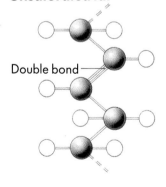

Double bond

⬤ Carbon

◯ Hydrogen

A fat consists of a fatty acid and GLYCEROL. Some fatty acids are essential for the healthy growth and development of the body, and need to be part of the diet. Fats that contain as many hydrogen atoms as they can are called saturated fats. Research has shown that saturated fats cause a build-up of CHOLESTEROL in the blood, which can lead to heart disease. Unsaturated and polyunsaturated fats, in which there are fewer hydrogen atoms, do not produce high cholesterol levels.

Natural fats are the raw materials for many manufacturing processes and go into the making of such products as margarine, soap and lipstick.

See also CARBOHYDRATES; NUTRITION; PROTEINS.

Fax

Facsimile transmission, or fax, is a system for sending information on paper by TELEPHONE lines. Fax is different from other COMMUNICATIONS systems such as telex and electronic mail. These transmit the information content of a document, but a fax machine transmits a copy of the document itself. It can, therefore, transmit drawings in addition to printed text. The first fax machines were ANALOGUE, but DIGITAL machines are becoming more common. Before a fax machine sends a document, it tests the telephone line it is going to use. If it detects a

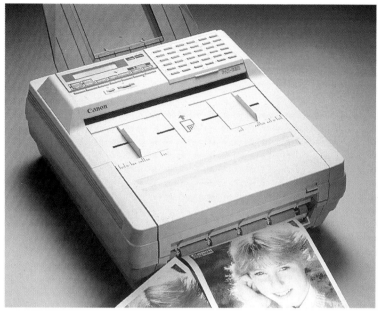

◀ A modern fax machine takes less than 30 seconds to transmit a one-page document.

▼ When the signals for a facsimile transmission arrive at the telephone receiver of the fax machine, the signals are separated from the carrier wave and fed into the printer. The printer recreates the document in horizontal chains of dots built up into lines.

bad line, one with interference and noise, it automatically switches to a slower data transmission speed. This reduces the risk of data being lost during transmission. The document is scanned and the image is converted into electrical signals. At the other end of the telephone line, another fax machine receives the signals, decodes them and prints out a copy of the original document. So that every fax machine in the world can decode the data sent by other fax machines, they must all use the same coding and decoding system.

Feathers

Feathers are found only on birds. They keep the birds warm and they also enable them to fly. Feathers are made of a horny material called keratin and they are extremely light. Each one consists of a hollow central shaft with lots of slender branches called barbs. The largest of the four main kinds of feathers are the *flight feathers* of the wings and tail. *Contour feathers* cover the body and the front edges of the wings, providing the smooth surface necessary for efficient flight. The contour feathers are like small flight feathers but they are more symmetrical. Underneath the contour feathers there is a layer of *down feathers* which keeps the bird warm. Scattered among the down feathers there are some tiny hairlike feathers, known as *filoplumes*. Connected to NERVES in the SKIN, they tell the bird when its feathers become

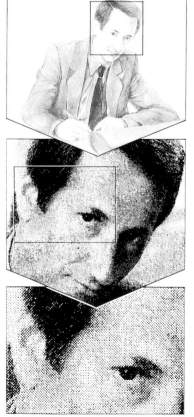

▶ *Water runs off a duck's back because the oil on the feathers makes them waterproof.*

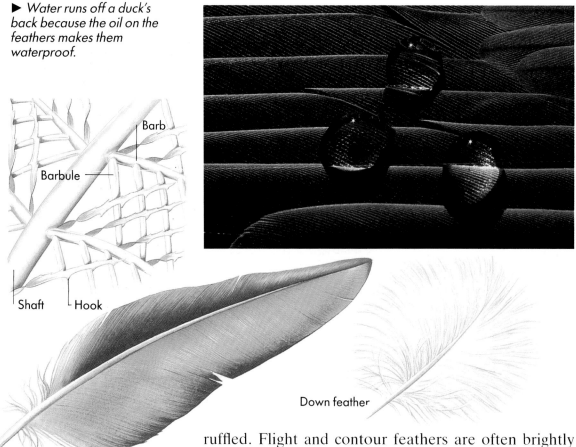

Barb

Barbule

Shaft   Hook

Down feather

Flight feather

▲ *Each feather has a hollow shaft running down its middle. Barbs grow out on either side, which are locked together in a crisscross pattern with tiny, hooked barbules. Under the flight feathers are down feathers, each with a short shaft and a tuft of fluffy barbs. These feathers trap a lot of air around the bird's body and keep it warm.*

ruffled. Flight and contour feathers are often brightly coloured, especially in the males, and they are used in DISPLAY to attract mates. Some of the colours are produced by PIGMENTS in the feathers, but others are produced by IRIDESCENCE.

See also AERODYNAMICS; HAIR; INSULATION, THERMAL.

Feedback

Feedback is a mechanism which allows an organism, or an electronic or mechanical system, to control its own processes. Feedback operates automatically, like the THERMOSTAT in a hot water system. In this case, the thermostat controls the heater, measuring the increasing temperature, and switching off the heat when it reaches the pre-set point. In a living organism, the same method switches CHEMICAL REACTIONS on and off. For example, a stimulus may cause an ENZYME to be produced. When the body detects that the enzyme has reached the proper level, the process of feedback switches off the production of the enzyme. This is called *negative feedback*. In our own bodies, carbon dioxide is produced as a waste

Negative feedback

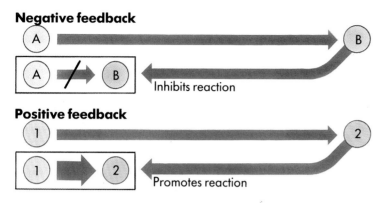

Inhibits reaction

Positive feedback

Promotes reaction

◀ *If **A** produces **B**, and the presence of more than a certain amount of **B** stops the reaction, it is negative feedback. If **1** produces **2**, and the presence of **2** keeps the reaction going, it is positive feedback.*

product. As this increases in CONCENTRATION, a *positive feedback* mechanism causes us to breathe more deeply, flushing out the carbon dioxide and increasing oxygen intake. All of the body's chemistry is ultimately controlled by these feedback mechanisms.

See also AUTOMATION; COORDINATION; METABOLISM.

Feeding

Plants and animals all need food in order to stay alive. The food provides the materials needed for GROWTH and the ENERGY needed for all the processes that go on inside the body. Plants make their own food by PHOTOSYNTHESIS, which uses the energy of sunlight to make SUGARS and other foods from water and carbon dioxide. Energy is locked up in these foods, and it passes to animals when they eat the plants.

Animals that eat plants are called *herbivores*. They include sheep, rabbits and many other grazing mammals, all of which have large molar TEETH for grinding up the vegetation. Many herbivores carry huge numbers of MICROORGANISMS inside their digestive canals to help them digest the plant material. This relationship of two organisms contributing to each other's welfare is an

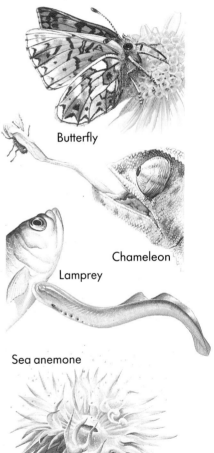

Butterfly

Chameleon

Lamprey

Sea anemone

▲ *These animals feed in very different ways. Butterflies suck nectar. Chameleons eat flies. Lampreys feed on other fish. Sea anemones filter particles from passing water.*

◀ *Lions hunt large prey. This zebra will provide food for the whole pride of lions.*

241

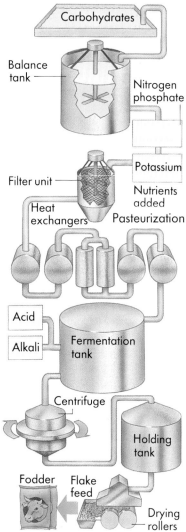

Production of fodder from carbohydrate waste

example of SYMBIOSIS. Animals that eat other animals are called *carnivores* and employ different methods for catching their prey. Some go out and hunt, whereas others lie in wait to ambush their prey. Carnivorous mammals have stabbing canine teeth for killing their prey, and sharp-edged cheek teeth for slicing meat.

Animals that eat both plant and animal matter are called *omnivores*. They include bears, badgers and humans. Scavengers, such as vultures and dung beetles, feed mainly on dead animals or their droppings. Many water-living animals, including mussels and other bivalves and many worms, feed by filtering tiny plants or animals or particles of dead matter from the water. These animals are called filter feeders.

See also DIGESTION; FOOD CHAIN; NUTRITION; PARASITE.

Fermentation

Fermentation is a biochemical process in which MICROORGANISMS such as bacteria, moulds, fungi and YEASTS break down an organic COMPOUND (consisting of carbon, hydrogen and oxygen). Fermentation is the basic process used in the production of alcoholic beverages such as beer, wine and cider. Yeast reacts with SUGAR to turn it into ALCOHOL and bubbles of CARBON DIOXIDE. During the 20th century, fermentation has also been used to make ANTIBIOTICS and other important DRUGS. For example, moulds act on mixtures of inorganic salts and molasses to make penicillin, a vital medicine. Modern BIOTECHNOLOGY relies on a kind of fermentation to produce many of the materials used in GENETIC ENGINEERING. Fermentation is also important in

▲ The waste products from a sweet-making factory are made into animal feeds by using a fermentation process. Carbohydrates are collected. Nutrients are added, the liquid is pasteurized and then fermented. Temperature and acidity are controlled to enable the yeast to grow. The liquid is drained off and the yeast cream is dried to produce animal fodder.

► During fermentation the yeast used to make beer rises to the top of the tanks.

making many kinds of bread, cheese and yoghurt.

Not all fermentation is useful. If MILK is allowed to ferment, the bacteria it contains turn it sour. Though fermentation has been used for centuries in brewing and baking, the part played by microorganisms was first discovered by the 19th-century French scientist Louis Pasteur. *See also* PASTEURIZATION.

Fermi, Enrico *See* Neutron

Fertilization

Almost all plants and animals begin life when a male CELL, or sperm, joins with a female cell, or EGG, of the same species. This joining of cells is called fertilization. In most animals the male cells fertilize the eggs inside the female's body after mating, but fertilization of many water-living animals takes place outside the body; the males scatter their sperm over the eggs after the females have laid them. Fertilization in FLOWERS takes place when male cells from the POLLEN grains join with egg cells in the ovary after pollination. After fertilization each egg grows into an EMBRYO and then into a completely new plant or animal. The fertilized egg contains genetic 'instructions' from both parents, so the new individual has some features from each.
See also CHROMOSOMES AND GENES; REPRODUCTION.

▼ *Fertilization in flowering plants starts when a grain of pollen lands on the stigma of a flower. The pollen grain makes a path to the ovary of the flower. The male gametes (sex cells) from the pollen travel down the path. One of the gametes fuses with the egg cell to form a fertilized egg.*

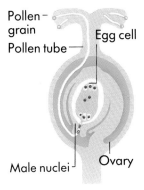

Pollen grain
Egg cell
Pollen tube
Male nuclei
Ovary

▼ *During spawning the female salmon lays up to 10,000 eggs. The eggs are fertilized by the male's sperm. A sperm makes enzymes so it can get through the outer membrane of the egg cell. The sperm then fuses with the egg's nucleus.*

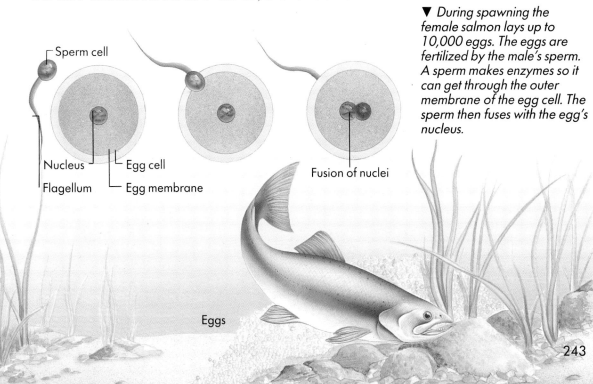

Sperm cell
Nucleus
Flagellum
Egg cell
Egg membrane
Fusion of nuclei
Eggs

243

▲ *The fields on either side of this ditch have been treated with fertilizers. The excess nutrients have drained off into the ditch, where they have encouraged the growth of algae and surface plants, such as duckweed, which completely cover the surface of the water. The resulting shortage of oxygen prevents the growth of water lilies and other plants and animals that normally grow there.*

Fertilizers

Fertilizers are chemicals added to the SOIL in order to improve the size and quantity of food crops, flowers and other plants. Plants make food for GROWTH by PHOTOSYNTHESIS. As well as sunlight, this process needs large amounts of certain ELEMENTS and tiny 'trace' amounts of others. These elements are required for NUTRITION, so they are called *nutrients*. Carbon, hydrogen, NITROGEN and oxygen come from the air and water in the ENVIRONMENT. Plants must absorb the other elements, such as calcium, sulphur, PHOSPHORUS and magnesium, from the soil. If the soil does not contain enough nutrients then the plants will not grow well. Farmers and gardeners can add fertilizers to provide the missing elements. Food production throughout the world is so important that fertilizer manufacture is a multi-million-pound industry. Too much fertilizer, however, can cause pollution. The increased CONCENTRATION of some elements can affect animal life as well.

Mineral fertilizers are the most widely used. They supply nitrogen, phosphorus and POTASSIUM to the soil. Nitrogen fertilizers, produced mainly from AMMONIA, include ammonium nitrate and ammonium phosphate. Fertilizer manufacturers use naturally-occurring potassium chloride to make potassium fertilizers. Natural fertilizers include decayed plant matter, animal waste (manure) and sewage. They have a lower concentration of nutrients than mineral fertilizers and therefore need to be used in larger quantities.

SEE FOR YOURSELF
Take 3 plant seedlings and water them every day. For the first use ordinary tap water. Water the second also with tap water, but once a week add a few drops of liquid fertilizer, carefully following the instructions on the bottle. Give water and fertilizer to the third plant every day. After a week or so you will see the effects of no fertilizer and too much fertilizer on seedlings 1 and 3.

Fibre optics *See* Optical fibres

Fibres, natural

Natural fibres are threads obtained from animals and plants. The fibres are spun into yarn which can then be woven on a loom to make cloth. The most commonly used animal fibre is sheep's wool. The quality of the cloth depends on which breed of sheep the wool came from. Other animals whose hair is used to make cloth include goats, alpacas and rabbits. Silk is the only major natural fibre to be obtained from an insect. Silkworms spin a cocoon to prepare for their transformation into moths. The long fibres are obtained by unwinding the threads from the cocoon.

More fibres are obtained from plants than animals. Cotton fibres come from a hairy clump around the head of the cotton plant. Jute, sisal and hemp are strong plant fibres that are used to make ropes and canvas. Linen is made from the stem fibres of flax. Fibres obtained from wood and grass are used to make paper and cardboard. Cellulose is extracted from plant CELL walls to make paper and synthetic materials.

See also CELLULOSE; SYNTHETIC FIBRES.

Cotton

Silk

Wool

Flax

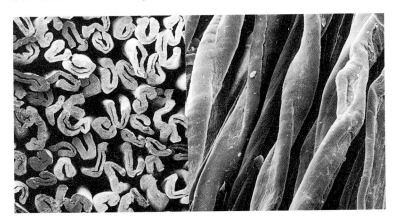

▲ Cotton is the most widely used natural fibre. The strongest, however, is silk. It is used for clothing and decorative fabrics.

◄ The different highly magnified shapes are cotton fibres, seen from their ends and side on. Cotton fibres do not have as many jagged edges as wool fibres, which is why cotton cloth feels smoother than wool.

◄ These wool fibres are shown magnified many times. The structure of wool fibres is similar to that of human hair.

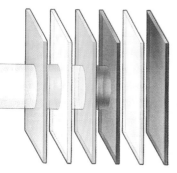

▲ *Colour film is made up of six layers. One is an emulsion that records blue light, the second absorbs excess blue light, the third records green light and the fourth records red light. The fifth, a plastic base, supports the emulsions. The last is a special backing that absorbs any remaining light.*

▶ *Developing and printing a black and white film: **1** the film is taken out of its case and wound round a special holder. This is done in a dark room. The film is placed inside a tank. Chemicals known as developer, stop bath and fixer are added in turn for carefully measured periods of time **2**. Next **3**, the film is washed to remove the chemicals after they have done their job. Finally, the film is removed from the tank and hung up to dry. When the film has been developed, the images are known as negatives **4**; the light areas of a subject appear dark and the dark areas appear light. The negative is placed on a holder below the lens of an enlarger **5**. Light is shone through the negative, which is enlarged onto the paper below it **6**. Darker areas of the negative let through less light and light areas let through more. The print is then developed and fixed in the same ways as the film **7** and washed and dried on a heated metal flat bed or hung up **8**.*

Film, photographic

Film is used in PHOTOGRAPHY for recording images. It consists of a strip of flexible plastic coated with a light-sensitive layer known as the emulsion. Holes punched along each edge of the film engage with toothed wheels called sprockets in the CAMERA. The first photographs were recorded on rigid plates. Flexible film made from CELLULOSE was introduced during the 19th century but cellulose-based film used to shoot the earliest movies is now breaking down. The PLASTIC base used in modern film is more stable. Film may be colour or black and white, for making prints or slides. When print film is developed, the result is a negative image, which must then be turned into a positive image by printing it on photographic paper. When slide film is developed, it produces a positive image on the film itself.

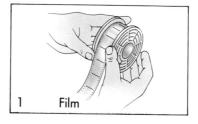

1   Film

5   Enlarger

2

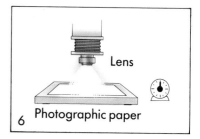

Lens

6   Photographic paper

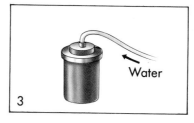

Water

3

7   Developer

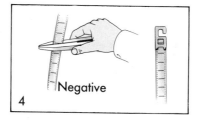

Negative

4

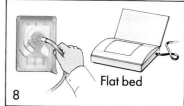

Flat bed

8

Filter, electronic

An electronic filter is a device used in a CIRCUIT to select which FREQUENCIES of an electromagnetic signal pass through to the rest of the circuit and which are blocked. Filters are used in RADIO transmission and reception. A low-pass filter allows all frequencies to pass through up to a certain cut-off frequency. All frequencies above the cut-off point are blocked. A high-pass filter allows all frequencies from a certain cut-off frequency (above zero) upwards to pass through. These filters can be used in HI-FI systems to eliminate low pitched rumbles, high pitched whistles and other sorts of distortion when playing music. Linking a high-pass filter and a low-pass filter together and choosing their cut-off frequencies carefully can produce other types of filter. A band-pass filter blocks everything below a lower cut-off and above a higher cut-off frequency. A band-elimination filter allows all frequencies below the lower and above the higher cut-off frequency to pass through, while the band between them is blocked.

See also ELECTRONICS.

▼ *Electronic filters are used to filter certain frequencies out of a band width of radio waves. A high-pass filter allows high frequencies through but masks out low frequencies. A low-pass filter allows low frequencies through but blocks out high frequencies. Together the two filters enable a particular frequency band to be selected.*

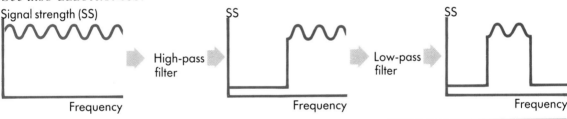

Filtration

Filtration is the process of removing SOLID impurities from a GAS or LIQUID by passing the gas or liquid through a filter. For example, you can separate a mixture of sand and water by pouring the mixture through a filter paper. The filter paper acts like a sieve and traps the solid particles of sand while allowing the water through. The liquid that is allowed to pass through a filter is called the *filtrate*. The solid material trapped by the filter is called the *residue*. In vehicle engines, a filter is used to remove impurities from the air entering a carburettor. Filtration equipment at water treatment works purifies drinking water from rivers and reservoirs before it is passed on to the WATER SUPPLY.

Different types of filtering materials are used in filtration processes. Filters made of sand or crushed

SEE FOR YOURSELF
Cut the top off a plastic bottle. Turn it upside-down and place it in the bottom half of the bottle. Put in a coffee filter and layers of wet sand and powdered charcoal. Pour some muddy water through the filter. The water becomes cleaner as it drips through.

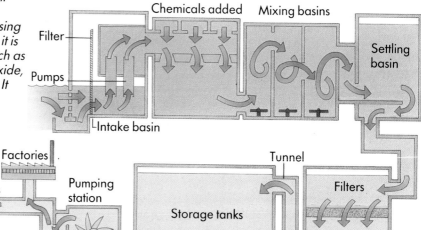

▼ Water takes about eight hours to pass through a filtration system. After passing through the system where it is treated with chemicals, such as chlorine and aluminium oxide, the water collects in wells. It then flows on to supply storage tanks.

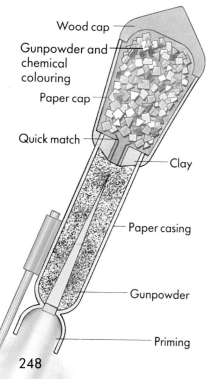

▼ A fuse is used to ignite the gunpowder in the body of the rocket. This produces a slow-burning explosion, which sends the rocket into the air.

Wood cap

Gunpowder and chemical colouring

Paper cap

Quick match

Clay

Paper casing

Gunpowder

Priming

charcoal are called granular filters. Filters may also be made of cloth or paper. Paper coffee filters have very tiny holes in them to allow water but not coffee grains to pass through. Filters made of membranes are commonly used in KIDNEY dialysis machines.

Fireworks

A firework is any of several devices in which GUNPOWDER or other combustible material is set alight to produce colourful effects or explosions. Fireworks are extremely dangerous if used incorrectly and should only ever be handled with great care. In many countries, the law forbids the sale of fireworks to children below a certain age. Other laws limit the amount and power of EXPLOSIVE that firms that make fireworks can use.

The ancient Chinese developed fireworks along with gunpowder for military purposes and for celebration or entertainment. The fireworks used in displays today are of various types. Most are made by packing a hollow tube with gunpowder and other COMPOUNDS that colour the flame or cause sparks. The powder is ignited by lighting a fuse. Firecrackers or 'bangers' simply make a loud noise, coloured fireworks contain ELEMENTS that burn to give distinctive colours. In a rocket, a lit fuse sets off a charge of coarsely ground gunpowder that releases gases behind the firework, propelling it into the air. Other fireworks in the rocket's nose are set off when the rocket reaches the top of its flight and produce colourful explosions. In a Roman candle, several gunpowder charges

248

are separated by non-explosive material to cause a series of small explosions and sparks. A Catherine wheel consists of a gunpowder-filled tube bent round a cardboard disc. Gases released by the BURNING gunpowder make the disc spin very rapidly.

Each chemical used to produce colour in fireworks gives off light of a characteristic colour.
White is produced by magnesium.
Red is produced by strontium compounds.
Green is produced by barium compounds.
Yellow is produced by sodium compounds.
Blue is produced by copper compounds.
Charcoal is also sometimes added; it gives a rocket a sparkling tail.

◀ *Colourful fireworks produced by harnessing various chemical reactions are often used in dramatic displays for public celebration.*

Fission, nuclear *See Nuclear physics*

Flame *See Combustion*

Flame test *See Analysis, chemical*

Flash point

The flash point of certain LIQUIDS is the lowest TEMPERATURE at which the VAPOUR above the liquid can be ignited in air. The vapour burns for a very short time, hence the term, flash point. Chemists apply the term mainly to liquid PETROLEUM products such as petrol. The flash point is in effect the lowest temperature at which a liquid such as petrol will burn, because below that temperature there is not enough vapour above the liquid's surface for COMBUSTION to take place. When storing or transporting flammable liquid such as petrol or paraffin which form a vapour easily, it is important to know the flash point for safety reasons.

Fleming, Alexander *See Antibiotic*

Firework Safety
All fireworks are dangerous. All fireworks burn vigorously, many explode and most are made of poisonous chemicals.
- At a firework display, keep fireworks in a metal box with a tight-fitting lid.
- Keep the box well away from a bonfire and the place where you let off the fireworks.
- Only open the box to take out a firework. Keep it closed at all other times.
- Never carry fireworks in your pocket.
- Never try to light fireworks with a match or cigarette lighter. Use a special glowing rope fuse.
- Never hold lit fireworks in your hand.
- If a firework's fuse goes out before the firework goes off, leave it alone. Do not approach it and do not try to re-light it.

FLIGHT ⚙

The earliest attempts to achieve human flight which imitated birds by using flapping wings were all unsuccessful.

The first successful human flights were made by balloon using the principle that a bag full of warm air would float upwards. In October 1783, two French brothers called Montgolfier sent up two friends in a hot-air balloon. In 1852, a Frenchman, Henri Giffard, made the first flight of a steerable balloon with a steam-engine driven propeller.

This was the forerunner of the airship: a rigid container or envelope full of hydrogen gas, propelled by engines and carrying a passenger compartment or gondola. The gas-filled envelope, being lighter than air, floated upwards. After a series of accidents in the 1920s and 1930s when the gas caught fire, destroying the craft, airships became unpopular. Modern airships use helium gas, which is not flammable.

In 1903, at Kitty Hawk, North Carolina, USA, Orville Wright made the first powered flight in a heavier-than-air machine. When it was driven forwards, the difference in airflow above and below its specially shaped wings created an upward force called lift. This is the same principle that enables birds to fly. Modern aircraft use this principle.

Nowadays, there are many different types of aircraft, including vertical take-off aircraft, fighters, bombers, passenger airliners, small business jets, airships, flying boats, private planes flown by aviation enthusiasts, helicopters and a range of different experimental aircraft.

◄ *A bird has a specialized body for flight including feathers, wings and strong, hollow bones.*

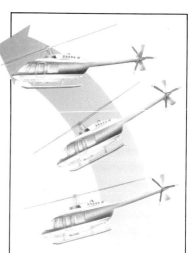

Helicopters do not need runways because they can take off vertically. They do this by spinning a set of thin wing-shaped rotor blades at high speed to create lift.

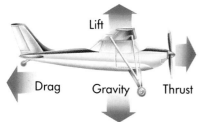

Lift

Drag   Gravity   Thrust

◄ *To fly, aircraft need power from their engines. They need lift provided by the wings, to raise them from the ground and to keep them in the air. The forward thrust of the engines balances the resistance, or drag, set up by the air.*

Milestones in the History of Flight
1492 Leonardo da Vinci draws concept of a flying machine.
1890 Adler's *Eole* becomes first full-sized aircraft to leave the ground under its own power.
1903 Orville Wright makes first sustained powered flight.
1908 Orville Wright makes first aircraft flight lasting 1 hour.
1909 Farman completes first aircraft flight of 100 miles (161 km).
1913 Sikorsky builds and flies a 4-engine aircraft.
1939 Sikorsky builds first modern helicopter.
1947 First aircraft flies at supersonic speed in USA.
1970 First 'jumbo jet' Boeing 747 brought into service.
1986 Rutan and Yeager pilot aircraft *Voyager* round the World without refuelling in a 9-day flight.

George Cayley (1773–1857)
A British engineer, Cayley is known for the many ideas he contributed to the early history of aviation, and is often called the father of modern aeronautics. He invented the biplane and built a glider that travelled 270 m. He wrote about helicopters, parachutes and streamlining the design of aircraft.

See also AERODYNAMICS; AIR; BALLOON; HYDROGEN; JET PROPULSION; TECHNOLOGY; WRIGHT, ORVILLE AND WILBUR.

Flotation

A body floats in a FLUID if the upward BUOYANCY force that it receives from the fluid is great enough to overcome the downward force of its WEIGHT. The upward force occurs because the PRESSURE in the fluid increases the deeper one goes, so that the upward pressure force on the bottom of the body is greater than the downward pressure force on the top. The principle of ARCHIMEDES states that the upward force is equal to the weight of the fluid which is displaced, or pushed out of the way, by the object. For an object to float, this upward force must balance the weight. This occurs if the object has a lower average DENSITY than the fluid, otherwise the fluid displaced will always be lighter than the object. Heavy ships float because they displace a large weight of water.

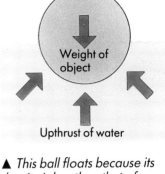

▲ This ball floats because its density is less than that of water. Only things that have a lower density than water can float in water.

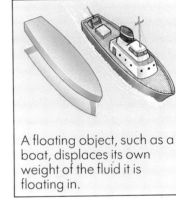

A floating object, such as a boat, displaces its own weight of the fluid it is floating in.

◄ An unladen ship rides high in the water.

SEE FOR YOURSELF
To investigate flotation, put some raisins in the bottom of a clear plastic beaker. Fill the beaker half full of clear, fizzy drink, such as lemonade. The raisins will begin to zoom up and down the beaker. Look at the gas bubbles that stick to the raisins. Bubbles of carbon dioxide gas from the fizzy drink collect on the raisins. The bubbles are lighter than the drink and lift the raisins to the surface. There, some of the gas escapes into the air. The raisins are too heavy for the remaining bubbles to support and so they sink to the bottom again.

FLOWERS

Most of the plants around us have flowers at some time. The flowers contain the plants' reproductive organs which produce seeds. A typical flower has a number of sepals around the outside. They protect the flower bud and may fall off when the bud opens. The most obvious parts of the flower are the petals. These are often brightly coloured and they attract insects to the flowers for pollination. The petals of a flower may be all alike or of several different shapes, as in the sweet pea and the snapdragon. Inside the petals, there are a number of pin-like stamens. These are the male parts of the flower which produce pollen. In the centre of the flower are one or more carpels, often joined together. These are the female parts containing the egg cells, or ovules, which eventually form the seeds. Everything is attached to the receptacle, which is the swollen top of the flower stalk.

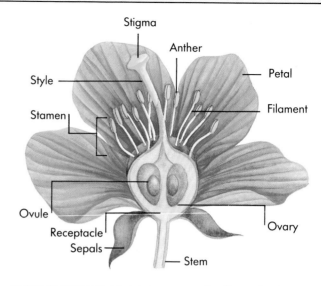

▲ This flower has been cut in half to reveal the main parts. Most flowers contain both stamens and carpels (male and female parts). The anther produces and stores the pollen. The stigma receives the pollen grains and it is here they germinate.

◄ The Lady's Slipper Orchid is one of Britain's most endangered plants. If people pick it the species could die out completely.

SEE FOR YOURSELF
Carefully pull a rose or other flower to pieces. See if you can identify the petals, stamens, sepals and the carpel, which is found at the bottom of the stigma, the central piece of the flower.

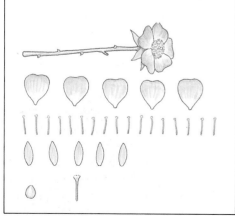

Bilaterally symmetrical flower

Composite flower

Flower with fused petals

▲ Bilaterally symmetrical flowers are not circular and have their structures arranged equally on both sides of a line. Composite flowers, like those of dahlias and daisies, are really many small flowers arranged in circles. The petals of some flowers are fused at their margins forming a tubular flower. Even prickly cactuses have flowers.

Cactus flower

See also BOTANY; COLOUR; EGGS; ENDANGERED SPECIES; FERTILIZATION; FRUIT; POLLEN AND POLLINATION; REPRODUCTION; SEEDS.

Fluid

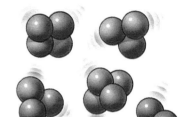

Together, LIQUIDS and GASES are known as fluids. At room temperature water is a fluid and a liquid, air is a fluid and a gas. Solids keep a definite shape by resisting forces (shear forces) that try to change their shape, or deform them. Fluids can flow to fill a container of any shape. This is because the MOLECULES which make up the fluid are able to move quite freely past each other, rather than being held rigidly to each other by the forces between them, as they are in a solid. Because they can change shape, or deform, to fill a different-shaped space, fluids are useful in driving machinery. In a vehicle's braking system, for example, the braking force is transmitted from the driver's brake pedal to the brake pads through the PRESSURE in a liquid (known as the brake fluid).

▲ Fluids flow easily. Any force or pressure will change the shape of a fluid. It will return to its former shape when the pressure is removed.

Fluorescence *See Luminescence*

Flywheel

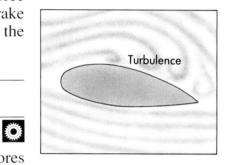

A flywheel is a heavy wheel spinning on a shaft. It stores ENERGY which is released when needed. Once a flywheel is spinning, it slows down very slowly. Some ENGINES produce an uneven POWER output. This can be smoothed out by fitting a flywheel to the engine's output shaft. When the power output falls, the flywheel keeps spinning until the power level rises again. Vehicles, such as city buses, which have to start and stop frequently are inefficient. Some experimental vehicles have been fitted with extra flywheels that spin up to high speeds when the vehicle brakes. The stored energy is used to get the vehicle going again, saving power and FUEL.

A fluid can be used like a flywheel (a fluid flywheel). The engine spins a propeller-like

▲ Air is a fluid. When air flows round an object the air flow changes. The flow round an aircraft's wing is streamlined until the aircraft flies at a steep angle. Then the air flow becomes turbulent, increasing the drag.

▶ This mid 18th-century steam locomotive plough has a fly-wheel fitted to the side of its boiler. The flywheel ensured that the plough had a constant amount of power passed to it by the engine.

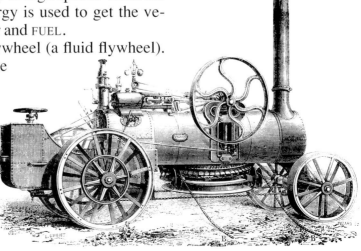

▶ The force of the water as the waves crash onto the shore traps air which forms foam full of millions of tiny bubbles. The foam looks like soap suds.

device called an impeller sealed inside a fluid-filled container. The fluid is forced to rotate with the impeller and its movement is transferred to a rotor on the vehicle's transmission system.

Foam

A foam is a COLLOID consisting of GAS bubbles scattered evenly throughout a LIQUID. Solid spongy materials are also called foams. A typical liquid foam is formed when air bubbles are forced into egg whites by whisking. A folding motion with a spoon or fork is used to keep the air in the liquid. Whipped cream is also a foam.

Foams are extremely useful. One consisting of bubbles of carbon dioxide in a non-flammable liquid is used in fighting petrol or oil fires. Foams do not last long in nature because the gas bubbles eventually group together and separate from the liquid. Stabilizers are used to make the foam last longer. Typical stabilizers are PROTEINS (used in foods such as marshmallows and whipped cream) and SOAP.

Foam rubber

Foam rubber is a spongy rubber which is full of air BUBBLES. Originally rubber was made from latex, the sap of some kinds of trees, but now it is usually made artificially. Foam rubber is made by blowing air through the liquid rubber to make it FOAM. It is then left to set. The end product is foam rubber which is used to make sponges and, in furniture manufacturing, to make the

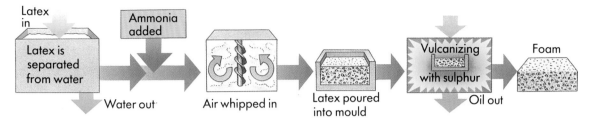

Latex in · Latex is separated from water · Ammonia added · Water out · Air whipped in · Latex poured into mould · Vulcanizing with sulphur · Oil out · Foam

padding in chairs and cushions. A chemical called a blowing agent can be mixed with the liquid. It gives off a gas, forming tiny bubbles in the liquid. This type of foam rubber is not absorbent like a sponge. It is used as a layer of insulation between materials or spaces at different temperatures, for example, in refrigerators, and to line the frames of doors and windows to prevent cold draughts.

▲ *Foam rubber is made by whipping air into latex. Some foam rubber may be as much as 90 percent air. After being poured into a mould it is left to set, after which it is vulcanized. Rubber is vulcanized by having sulphur added to it while it is heated. This makes the rubber stronger and more elastic.*

Focus

A focus is a place where, for example, a beam of LIGHT is brought together to pass through a single point. This is often done by using a LENS; the light is bent when it passes from the air into the lens and bent again when it passes back from the lens to the air. The light is bent towards the focus of the lens. The *focal length* of a lens is the distance of the focus from the centre of the lens. Lenses which bend light a lot (powerful lenses) have smaller focal lengths. Lenses are used to focus light in optical instruments such as MICROSCOPES and TELESCOPES. There is a lens in your EYE which focuses light so that you can see.

Mirrors can also focus light; a curved MIRROR will reflect light so that it passes through a focus.
See also REFLECTION; REFRACTION.

Focus can be used as a verb and a noun. *To focus* on something is to concentrate something, such as light or attention, on the object. *The focus* is the place where the light, or attention, is focused, and in the case of a lens where an image is *in focus*. **Foci** is the plural of focus.

▼ *A converging lens brings an inverted image into focus in the image plane. In a camera, the film is in the image plane.*

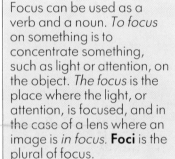

Incoming light · Focal point · Parallel rays of light · Converging lens · Lens focused for object 1 · Inverted image

◄ *The lens used to take this photograph was focused on the central bulb.*

255

Fog

Fog consists of tiny droplets of water suspended in AIR close to the ground surface. Such a cloud-like blanket of fog may reduce the visibility dramatically, especially if the fog forms at night. When visibility has been reduced to less than 1 km, it is called fog but if visibility is greater than 1 km, then it is often referred to as 'mist'.

Fog usually occurs when the air near to ground level is almost saturated with water VAPOUR. Fogs are caused when the air containing large amounts of water vapour is cooled suddenly, such as when it comes into contact with the cold ground. Fog is more likely to occur in areas where there is a high level of AIR POLLUTION, because the water vapour is more likely to condense around the particles in the ATMOSPHERE. Fog containing smoke is often called 'smog'.

▼ Advection fog forms when warm, moist air travels over a cool surface, or when cold air passes over warm water. Frontal fog forms where two air masses of different temperatures meet. Radiation fog forms at night in low places as the Earth's heat escapes upwards, leaving cool air at ground level. As the temperature drops fog is formed. Upslope fog forms as moist air cools when it travels up a slope.

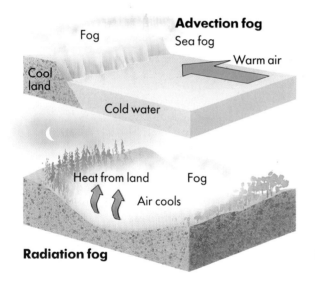

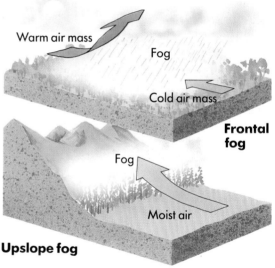

Food additives

Food additives are any of a group of substances that are added to processed foods by the manufacturers. They include colourings, preservatives, anti-oxidants (to stop food reacting with oxygen in the air), emulsifiers and stabilizers (to control the fat content of the food), sweeteners, solvents and flavour enhancers (to stimulate the taste buds) and added VITAMINS. Some food additives are natural materials such as salt and sugar which have been used for thousands of years. Modern CHEMISTRY has given rise to a large number of artificial food additives.

Some flavouring agents added to food add no flavour of their own, but improve a food's natural flavour. Monosodium glutamate is one of these agents. It is a white crystalline substance that improves the taste of meats, vegetables, soups, etc and is often used in Chinese food.

Food additives		Possible adverse effects
Tartrazine (artificial colouring)	E102	Skin rashes, breathing problems, blurred vision, purple patches on skin, hyperactivity in children.
Potassium nitrate (preservative)	E252	Severe stomach pain, vomiting, muscular weakness, irregular pulse.
Butylated hydroxytoluene (anti-oxidant)	E321	Skin rashes, hyperactivity in children.
Monosodium glutamate (flavour enhancer)	E621	Headaches, dizziness, neck pains, muscular weakness.

Some food additives have caused concern because of their apparent connection with health problems. Tartrazine, for example, is an artificial yellow colouring that has been linked with skin rashes and hyperactivity in children. Monosodium glutamate, a flavour enhancer made from sugar beet and wheat, has been linked to headaches and dizziness in some people. The vast majority of food additives are thought to be harmless. Some are harmless to healthy adults, but may cause problems in children or people with certain medical problems such as disorders of the kidneys. In Europe, each permitted food additive is given an 'E' number which appears in the list of ingredients on the packaging.
See also FOOD PRESERVATION.

◀ *Artificial substances used in food must satisfy strict regulations regarding their effect on people. Many substances are no longer used as food colourings because their effects are known to be harmful.*

Food chain

Rabbits eat grass: foxes eat rabbits. This is a simple food chain or ENERGY chain. All animals belong to food chains because they depend on other ORGANISMS for their food and energy. If you upset one part of a food chain, you will unbalance it. *See pages 258 and 259.*

FOOD CHAIN

All animals depend ultimately on green plants. These plants are known as producers, because only they can produce energy-giving food, by photosynthesis, from non-living matter. The next link in the chain must be a herbivore or plant-eater. It gets all its energy from the plants that it eats and is known as a primary consumer. The rabbit is the primary consumer in the simple chain: rabbits eat grass, foxes eat rabbits. The next animal in the chain is a carnivore or flesh-eater. It gets its energy by eating the primary consumer and is known as a secondary consumer. There may be one or even two more carnivores further up the chain, and the one at the top is called the top predator. The higher up food chains you go, the fewer animals you will find. On the African savanna, for example, there are about 100 gazelles for every lion, and those gazelles require millions of grass plants (over 250 hectares of grassland) to keep them alive. There are rarely more than five links in a food chain, because energy is used up at each stage just to keep the animals alive. There would not be enough energy to go round if there were too many links in the chain.

Most animals eat more than one kind of food and belong to several different food chains. The chains in any particular habitat are thus linked together to form a food web. All the energy passing through the system comes originally from the Sun, trapped by the plants during photosynthesis.

The lanner falcon, the caracal, the lion and the leopard are the top predators on the plains and they have no real enemies, but the food chains do not stop there. When these animals die a host of scavengers, including the vultures, will eat the dead bodies.

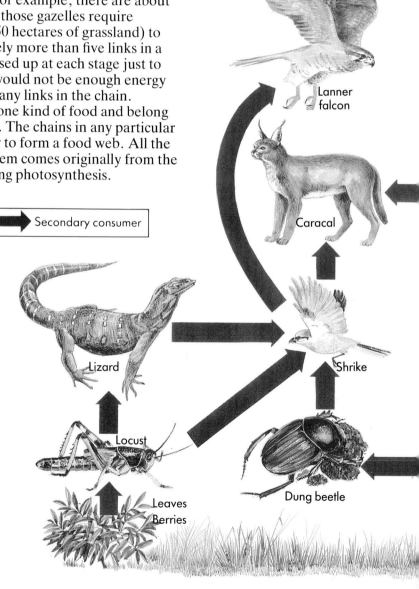

Lanner falcon

Caracal

Shrike

Lizard

Locust

Leaves
Berries

Dung beetle

Producer ➡ Primary consumer ➡ Secondary consumer

▲ In any food chain the producer is always a plant. This plant is fed upon by a herbivore or primary consumer which is eaten by a carnivore or secondary consumer.

▶ This is a small part of the food web on the African savanna. There are three main food chains, in which the primary consumers are the locust, the antelope and the hare. You can see that the chains are linked by many cross-connections before they reach the top predators, but everything begins with the plants. The antelope produce dung, which is eaten by dung beetles and other insects. Each organism depends on the others. If the grass dies there will be nothing for the antelope to feed on so they will move away to try and find food. The lions and vultures will follow the antelope or eat more of different types of animal.

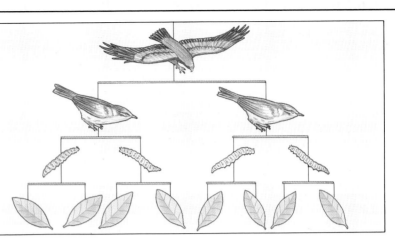

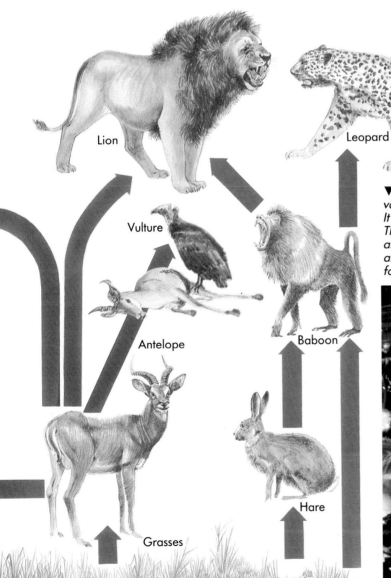

Lion

Leopard

Vulture

Antelope

Baboon

Grasses

Hare

▼ *Plankton is the name given to the great variety of marine and freshwater organisms. It consists of microscopic plants and animals. They serve as a primary food source for animals, such as jellyfish, molluscs, sponges and certain fish. These in turn provide food for larger fishes.*

See also ECOLOGY; ECOSYSTEM; ENERGY; ENVIRONMENT; FEEDING; MICROORGANISMS; NUTRITION; ORGANISM; PHOTOSYNTHESIS; SUN.

Preventing Poisoning

The following precautions can help to prevent food poisoning:

- Choose the food you buy carefully, making sure that it is fresh.
- Wash your hands before you touch food and be sure you do not have any open cuts or skin infections.
- Wash fruit and vegetables.
- Refrigerate foods that spoil easily.
- Never eat raw or undercooked pork and chicken.

▶ *Greatly magnified using an electron microscope, this photograph shows the bacterium* Salmonella enteritidis. *This bacterium has been found to be a cause of food poisoning. It has been associated with infected hens' eggs and poultry.*

Irradiation is a method of preserving food. It involves bombarding food with gamma radiation, X-rays or accelerated electrons to kill the microorganisms that make food decay.
Only some countries have allowed irradiation to be used for food preservation, others are not yet satisfied that it is entirely effective.

Food poisoning

Food poisoning can be caused by the presence of certain types of bacteria, or by substances (POISONS or toxins) that they produce, in our food. It may cause no more than temporary diarrhoea or vomiting, but is sometimes very serious. Bacteria in food are difficult to detect, because they do not always cause a smell of decay. Food poisoning is usually caused by contamination during food processing, or by incorrect storage methods.

Salmonella is a very common bacterium found in poultry. Chickens need careful cooking to prevent the salmonella increasing in number and causing a health

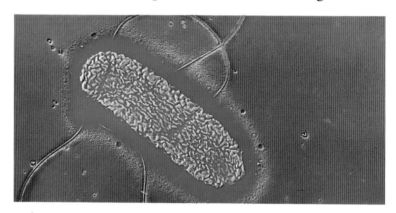

risk. The meat must be cooked properly and no utensil that was used for the uncooked meat should be used for the cooked meat. Salmonella can even enter eggs. Listeria is another bacterium which is found in certain types of cheese. It can be dangerous to people who are not strong, the elderly, young children and particularly to pregnant women. It can continue to grow at the low temperatures used for storing precooked foods. Staphyllococcus can be spread when a food handler has a skin infection like boils. Botulism is caused by a toxin released from the Clostridium bacteria, and can cause paralysis and death. Fortunately it is rare, and only occurs in poorly treated canned food. Food poisoning can be avoided by careful food storage and preparation.

Food preservation

Food preservation describes a range of methods used to prevent food from spoiling or decomposing. Without any form of preservation, MICROORGANISMS soon invade foods and make them inedible. People have been preserving food since prehistoric times. Traditional preservation methods include drying, smoking and salting, candying (sealing in a sugary coat) and pickling. Dried food is preserved because the microorganisms that spoil food cannot grow without moisture. Chemicals in the smoke used to smoke foods inhibit these organisms. Very salty and acid conditions have the same effect.

These methods are still used, but knowledge of the way that food-spoiling microorganisms grow and multiply has led to new methods including CANNING, FREEZING and a combination of freezing and drying, called FREEZE-DRYING. Nuclear technology offers another method, called irradiation. If food is exposed to RADIOACTIVITY, microorganisms living in the food are killed, greatly extending the shelf-life. Irradiation is still an experimental method and is not accepted by everyone.

▼ *It is important to keep food at a low temperature to preserve the food between the time it is produced and the time it is eaten. The food may be stored in a cold store after production. It is then transported in a refrigerated lorry to the supermarket where it is held in another cold store before being placed in the supermarket refrigerator. The consumer purchases the product and places it in his or her own fridge. Temperature change and much freezing and thawing can lead to deterioration in the food and cause the growth of microorganisms.*

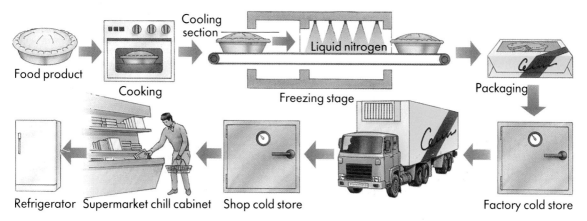

Food product — Cooking — Cooling section — Liquid nitrogen — Freezing stage — Packaging — Factory cold store — Shop cold store — Supermarket chill cabinet — Refrigerator

Force

A force is something that pushes or pulls an object in a particular direction. Isaac NEWTON realized that if one object produces a force on another, the first object experiences an equal and opposite reaction force. He also realized that forces cause objects to accelerate; to keep something moving in a straight line at a constant speed does not need a force, except to balance the force of FRICTION. When a force moves through some distance, for example, when you lift up a weight and put it on a table, the force does WORK and uses up ENERGY. When the object does not move no work is done and it takes no energy for the table to continue supporting the weight once you have put it there. A lever can be used to convert a small force into a large force; in order that the amount of work done by both forces is the same, the

SEE FOR YOURSELF
Drop a tennis ball and watch it bounce. The ball falls because of the pull of gravity. When it collides with a hard surface it changes direction.

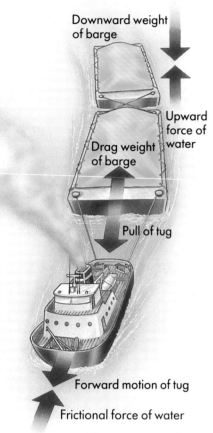

Downward weight
of barge

Upward
force of
water

Drag weight
of barge

Pull of tug

Forward motion of tug

Frictional force of water

▲ *Several forces act together on this tug and cargo. The frictional force of water acts against the direction of travel. The downward force of gravity on the barges acts against the upwards force of the water. The pull of the tug acts against the drag weight of the cargo.*

▶ *Evidence collected at the scene of the crime is analysed by forensic scientists in the laboratory. The results are used in the legal proceedings as part of the case brought against the accused.*

small force must be moved through a larger distance than the large force.

The force that pulls objects downwards towards the Earth is called GRAVITY, and the force of ELECTRICITY and MAGNETISM is called electromagnetic force.

Forensic science

Forensic science is used by police forces to provide technical information about a crime. It is the study of items associated with a crime, in order to deduce facts about them. For example, a forensic scientist will examine threads and fibres found at the site of a crime, to see if they match up with fibres associated with a suspect. Forensic scientists may also examine a bullet to see if its markings can identify the gun from which it was fired.

Forensic medicine provides evidence about individuals. It can tell how long it is since a person died, from the body TEMPERATURE, or can prove that a particular weapon was used. Finger printing is used to identify a person, because no two people have identical finger prints. Now there are techniques for the examination of blood and other body fluids that can identify a person.

Forging

Forging is a process for shaping METAL by hammering while it is still hot. When IRON or steel is heated to a high enough TEMPERATURE, it becomes soft and can be shaped. Until the 19th century, all forging was done by hand, usually by blacksmiths in forges. In 1839, the Scottish engineer James Nasmyth, invented a steam-powered hammer. A piece of metal formed by forging is less

brittle than one formed by CASTING. If a large number of identical metal parts are needed, they can be made by a process called drop-forging. A piece of metal is positioned between an anvil and a drop-hammer. The drop-hammer is a heavy metal block with a shaped 'die' on the bottom. It drops with great force onto the piece of metal, forming the part instantly.

See also DUCTILITY; MALLEABILITY.

> **Forging is probably the oldest method of shaping metal known. Metal was first forged over 6000 years ago. The first iron worked by forging was found in meteorites and in many early languages the word 'iron' meant 'metal from the sky'. By 1200 BC ironworkers could reheat, work and cool iron to make wrought iron with properties similar to those of some carbon steels today.**

Formula, chemical

A chemical formula is a shorthand method of writing down the ingredients of a chemical COMPOUND. Each ELEMENT has its own CHEMICAL SYMBOL. A formula uses the symbols with figures to show the proportions in which the elements combine to form the compounds. The *empirical formula* of a compound indicates the ATOMS of each element in the compound in their simplest RATIO. The empirical formula for ethene is CH_2. The *molecular formula* of a compound gives the numbers of each atom making up a single MOLECULE of that compound. The molecular formula for ethene is C_2H_4. This shows that two atoms of carbon combine with four atoms of hydrogen in an ethene molecule. The *structural formula* of a compound is a way of indicating the chemical bonds that hold the atoms together in the molecule.

Fossil

A fossil is any remains or trace, such as a shell, bone or a footprint, preserved in ROCK by gradually being changed into rock itself. These remains belonged to an animal or plant which lived a long time ago.

When an animal, for example, a cockle, dies in the sea

▼ *Chemical formulae are internationally agreed symbols that are used as a kind of shorthand for the names of chemical compounds. They show the different atoms of a molecule and sometimes how they are arranged.*

Structural formula
of ethene

$$H \diagdown \qquad \diagup H$$
$$C = C$$
$$H \diagup \qquad \diagdown H$$

or

$$CH_2 = CH_2$$

Molecular formula
of ethene

$$C_2H_4$$

▶ Scientists carefully chip away rock to reveal the fossilized bones of a huge dinosaur.

▼ Fossils form when animal or plant remains get covered with sediments that later turn to rock. **1** The animal dies and its body comes to rest on the bottom of a lake or the sea. **2** The soft parts of the body (the skin and muscles) rot leaving the bones of the skeleton. The bones are covered with mud and sand and gradually these sediments turn to rock. **3** After millions of years the landscape changes, and if the rock containing the fossil rises and is worn away the fossil can be seen.

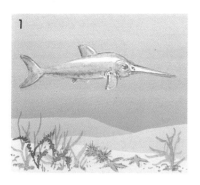

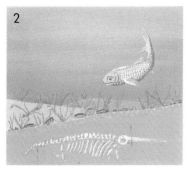

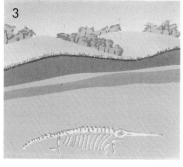

it sinks to the sea bed. There its soft parts will usually decay, but the cockle's shell may soon become buried by sediment. More sediment is deposited and eventually the silt or mud hardens into rock and the MINERALS in the rock are replaced until the fossil turns to a kind of rock itself different from the surrounding material.

Although millions of fossils have been found, they are very rare compared to the numbers of animals and plants which have lived since life on Earth first evolved 3000 million years ago. This is because the conditions in which fossilization can occur are rare. Most fossils are of sea organisms because fossilization is more likely to take place in the sea. If an animal dies on land, its flesh will be eaten and its SKELETON broken up before it could be covered with sediment that could harden into rock.

Fossil fuels

Fossil fuel is the name given to COAL, PETROLEUM and NATURAL GAS which are extracted from the rocks of the Earth's crust and used to provide the FUEL for heating and the generation of power such as ELECTRICITY. Many chemicals are also derived from petroleum. These fuels are made from the animal and plant remains which have formed FOSSILS, hence their name. Peat is not strictly a fossil fuel because most peat has been formed since the last Ice Age and is continuing to be formed today. Fossil fuels are HYDROCARBONS.

Natural gas and oil are often found together, with the gas occupying pores in the rocks at a higher level than the oil. Petroleum also occupies pores in permeable rocks that allow liquids to pass through them. They are often capped by an impermeable layer such as clay.

▼ Coal can be extracted from seams that lie near the surface by removing the topsoil to make an open-cast pit. Deeper seams are reached by shafts and tunnels. Anthracite, the hardest and best coal, is usually the deepest.

Open cast pit

Coal (lignite)
Sandstone
Shale
Coal (bituminous)

Coal (anthracite)

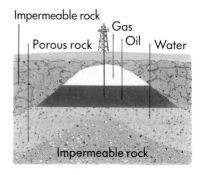

Impermeable rock

Porous rock

Gas
Oil
Water

Impermeable rock

▲ Oil-bearing rock holds drops of oil between its grains. It seeps up through porous rock, such as sandstone, until it is stopped by impermeable rock, such as granite.

Foucault pendulum

A Foucault pendulum is a PENDULUM that is free to swing in any direction. Once it has begun to swing in a particular direction, it will keep swinging to and fro in this direction unless it is disturbed by some outside FORCE. A pendulum like this can be used to detect the daily ROTATION of the EARTH, since all the surrounding objects will rotate with the Earth but the direction of the pendulum will not. It is named after Jean-Bernard Foucault (1819–1868), a French physicist who hung a brass ball weighing 137 kg on a 70 m-long wire from the dome of the Panthéon in Paris in 1851 and demonstrated that the Earth rotates once a day.

▶ A strong piece of string, at least 6 m long, hung from the top of a stairwell, with a heavy weight (at least 5 kg), attached to it, will show a change in its angle of swing during the day. The pendulum must be able to swing freely. The path of the pendulum can be marked at intervals to show the apparent changes of direction.

Thread (at least 6 m long)

Weight (at least 5 kg)

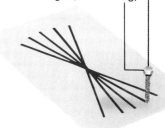

◀ A Foucault pendulum is designed to show the rotation of the Earth. It swings backwards and forwards in the same plane, but the rotation of the Earth makes the pendulum appear to change its path gradually over a period of several hours.

265

▲ Benjamin Franklin served the United States as a public leader, statesman and scientist.

Franklin, Benjamin

Benjamin Franklin (1706–1790) was an American printer, scientist, publisher and statesman who played an important part in the formation of the United States of America as a nation. Franklin was born in Boston, Massachusetts, the tenth son of 17 children. At 12 years he went to work for his brother, a printer in Philadelphia, but gave it up in 1748 to study science. He proved that LIGHTNING is electrical and later invented the LIGHTNING CONDUCTOR to protect buildings.

He came to England to try to settle some tax disputes but returned to the United States in 1775, before the American War of Independence. Franklin helped draft the Declaration of Independence and was one of those who signed the Constitution.

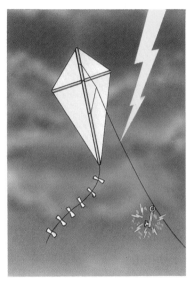

▲ Franklin flew a kite during a thunderstorm – a very dangerous thing to do – and proved that lightning is electricity. The electricity passed from a metal spike on the kite down the string to a metal key, where it produced sparks. He also invented the lightning conductor, bifocal glasses and a smokeless stove.

Lightning rod

Bifocal glasses

Franklin stove

Freeze-drying

Freeze-drying is a process used in FOOD PRESERVATION. One of the disadvantages of preserving food by drying it is that the flavour and appearance of the food can be impaired. The quality of the food can be improved if the drying time can be reduced as much as possible. One way is to freeze the food quickly in a VACUUM, freeze-drying. Freeze-drying is particularly successful with meat products. When a piece of meat is frozen in a vacuum, water in the meat cells turns to ice and then, because of the vacuum, it turns into VAPOUR. The ice formed in the meat cells has sublimed, gone from solid to vapour without becoming liquid in between.

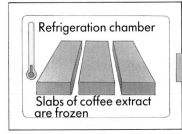

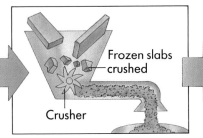

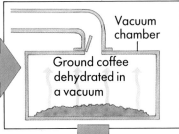

Refrigeration chamber

Slabs of coffee extract are frozen

Frozen slabs crushed

Crusher

Vacuum chamber

Ground coffee dehydrated in a vacuum

Freezing

Freezing describes the conversion of a material from its liquid or vapour state into its solid state by reducing its TEMPERATURE. Water, for example, normally exists as a liquid. If it is cooled, it eventually begins to change into a solid, ice. If ice is heated, it changes back to liquid. The temperature at which a material changes from a solid to a liquid is called its MELTING POINT.

Freezing is widely used in FOOD PRESERVATION. Frozen food does not decompose because the organisms responsible for spoiling food cannot grow in very low temperatures. A freezer uses a HEAT PUMP to transfer HEAT from the colder food cabinet to its warmer surroundings. Food was preserved in ancient Rome by packing it in ice, but the widespread use of freezing as a method of food preservation was not possible until the invention of REFRIGERATION in 1858 and a quick freezing process developed in the 1920s. Domestic freezers can now store food safely for several months or up to a year, depending on the freezer's temperature and whether the food is fresh or already frozen.

▲ *Freeze-dried instant coffee is made by freezing freshly made coffee extract into slabs. The slabs are ground and put into a vacuum chamber. Moisture in the form of ice is drawn off and dry crystals are left.*

The freezing point of nearly all liquids is lowered by adding another substance. This is shown quite dramatically when an antifreeze containing ethanediol (ethylene glycol) is added to the water in a car's cooling system. The water freezes at 0°C, the ethanediol freezes at −13°C, but a mixture of equal parts of water and ethanediol freezes at about −37°C!

◄ *Large woolly mammoths were common a million years ago. Dozens of deep-frozen mammoths have been dug up in almost perfect condition. This baby mammoth was found in Siberia in 1977.*

Freezing Points	
Carbon (diamond)	3750°C
Gold	1063°C
Hydrogen	–259°C
Mercury	–38.87°C
Silver	961°C
Tin	232°C

Heinrich Hertz (1857–1894)
Hertz was a German scientist. He was the first person to broadcast and receive radio waves. In 1883 he began working on electromagnetic radiation. He produced radio waves by using a rapidly oscillating electric spark and was able to measure their velocity and their wavelength. This confirmed the theory developed by James Clerk Maxwell. The unit of frequency, the hertz, was named after him. One hertz (1 Hz), is equivalent to one cycle or oscillation per second.

Freezing point

The freezing point of a substance is the TEMPERATURE at which it changes from a LIQUID to a SOLID. For pure substances consisting of a single element or a simple compound, the freezing point is the same as the MELTING POINT. Different substances have widely differing freezing points. The element bromine, which is a volatile liquid at room temperature, freezes at –7°C. Iron has a freezing point of 1539°C. Pure water freezes at 0°C. But impure water freezes at a lower temperature. Water in a vehicle engine is stopped from FREEZING in winter by the addition of ANTIFREEZE, which lowers the water's freezing point to –37°C.

Frequency

Frequency is a measure of how often a process repeats itself. Frequency is used to describe the motion of waves, in which case it states how often a complete cycle of the WAVE MOTION is gone through in a certain time. The SI UNIT of frequency is the HERTZ (Hz) which corresponds to one wave cycle every second. Electromagnetic waves of a wide range of frequencies are used; RADIO waves have frequencies of a few hundred thousand hertz or a few million hertz; LIGHT waves have frequencies of a several hundred million million hertz. Sound waves, which are waves of vibration in the air, have much lower frequencies than light; we can hear SOUND frequencies between about 20 Hz and 20,000 Hz. Musical notes correspond to different frequencies; 'middle C' has a frequency of 256 Hz.

The frequency of a wave is related to its WAVELENGTH; the wavelength multiplied by the frequency gives the speed of the wave, so for a given speed higher frequency waves have shorter wavelengths.

► Frequency (pitch) of sound is determined by the number of air vibrations per second. The greater the number of complete wave cycles, the higher the frequency and the higher the pitch. The loudness of a sound depends on the amplitude, the height of the waves.

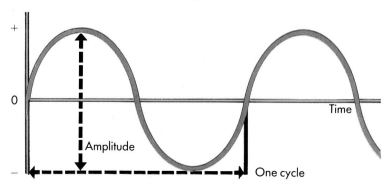

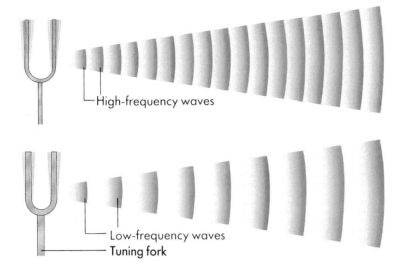

High-frequency waves

Low-frequency waves
Tuning fork

◀ *High notes have higher frequencies than low notes. The top tuning fork makes a note that is one octave (eight notes) higher than the note made by the bottom tuning fork. The note made by the top tuning fork has double the frequency of the bottom tuning fork. For example, C above middle C, is 512 Hz and middle C is 256 Hz.*

Frequency modulation *See* Radio

Freud, Sigmund

Sigmund Freud was born in Freiberg, then a part of the Austrian empire, in 1856. He was a neurologist who pioneered psychoanalysis, a technique for examining the motivations and hidden activities of the mind. Studying in Paris, Freud noted that, in patients suffering from hysteria, physical illness could also appear. This association of mind with body led him to study patients with mental disorders, and to develop psychoanalysis, in which patients were encouraged to tell him their dreams and deepest thoughts. Freud would prompt them to reconsider their dreams and earliest memories, in the belief that these had an effect on their current behaviour. In the early 20th century, his theories became extremely popular, having a lasting effect on art, literature, education and social attitudes. He died in London in 1939.

▲ *Freud is famous for his much debated theory, in which he said that unconscious motives control much of our behaviour.*

Friction

Friction is a FORCE which tends to stop objects sliding past each other. For example, if you try to push a heavy box of books across the floor, you have to push hard to overcome the friction between the box and the floor. Friction can be useful; for example, the friction between our shoes and the ground stops our feet sliding from under us when we push back with our feet to walk forward. Without friction, we could not walk or run. A car uses the friction between its tyres and the road in a

Friction can be a nuisance in machines, which need bearings and lubrication to overcome it. But friction also has important uses.
- It makes a railway locomotive's wheels grip the smooth steel rails.
- It makes car tyres grip the road surface.
- It makes the soles of our shoes grip the ground when we walk.
- It allows a conveyor belt to run on pulley wheels without slipping.
- It makes nails stay in wood when they are hammered in.

▶ *A vehicle's brakes rely on friction. In a disc brake, hydraulic pressure forces friction pads to squeeze a metal disc that rotates on the same axle as the wheel. Here a disc brake is being tested. The force of the friction is so great that the disc brake has become hot and is glowing. Parts of machines that may have to be subjected to high temperatures are often made of special heat-resistant metals or other materials.*

similar way. Friction can also cause problems; if two moving parts of a machine rub each other, the friction can cause them to wear away and become damaged. Friction and wear can be reduced by LUBRICATION, coating the surface with a substance such as oil which enables sliding to take place more easily. Ball BEARINGS or roller bearings are used in machines so that surfaces do not slide directly past each other.

Friction causes ENERGY to be lost in the form of HEAT because as materials rub together the molecules which make them up vibrate, producing heat energy.

Friction causes wasted energy in all machines. About one-fifth of the power used in the average car engine is wasted by friction of the moving parts.

SEE FOR YOURSELF
Arrange a selection of objects in a line along a piece of smooth wooden board. Amongst the objects include an ice-cube, a rubber and a toy car. Take hold of one end of the board and gradually lift it up. Make a note of which objects move first. The objects that move more easily do so because there is less friction between their outer surface (which is smooth) and the surface of the board.

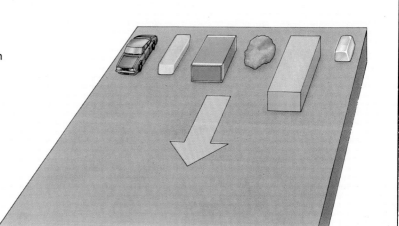

Front, weather

A weather front is the boundary between two masses of AIR at different TEMPERATURES and PRESSURES. One result of the difference in air pressure between two contrasting air masses is that a front is an area where the wind speed

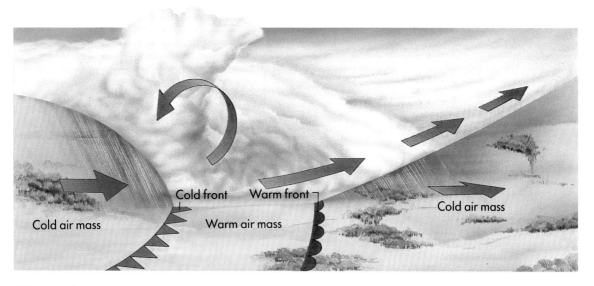

▲ A mass of warm air is enclosed between areas of cold air. At the warm air front (shown on a weather map by a curved line with solid semicircles on it), warm air rises over the cold air front (shown by a line with solid triangles), forming clouds.

◀ Thunderstorms occur when warm air, lying over a thin wedge of cold air, starts to rise quickly as the cold front advances.

may change very rapidly over quite a short distance.

There are three different kinds of fronts. In a warm front, the mass of warmer air moves over the mass of cooler air. As the warm front passes, the air temperature rises, rainfall decreases and, in the Northern Hemisphere, the wind veers south-west. In a cold front, cold air is moving under the mass of warm air. A cold front may bring with it a fall in air temperature and brighter weather with the wind, in the Northern Hemisphere, veering north-west. An occluded front forms when a warm front is overtaken by a cold one and the warm air is forced up.

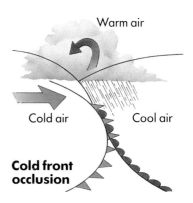

▲ Occluded fronts (shown by alternate solid semicircles and triangles) are a sandwich of cold air with warm air in the middle or cold air sandwiched by warm air.

Fruit

A fruit is the part of a plant which contains the SEEDS. Fruits develop from the carpels of FLOWERS, usually after FERTILIZATION. The fruits protect the seeds in the early stages, and when the seeds are ripe the fruits often help to scatter them. *See* pages 272 and 273.

FRUIT

The objects pictured below are all fruits. Ripe fruits are of two main kinds, dry ones and juicy ones. The poppy capsule and the pea pod are dry fruits with several or many seeds. They split open when they are ripe to allow the seeds to escape. The acorn is a single-seeded dry fruit and it does not split open: the germinating seeds simply force their way through the fruit walls. The tomato and the marrow are berries. Berries are juicy fruits containing several seeds. The cherry is a drupe, also called a stone fruit because the inner layer of the fruit forms a woody 'stone'. The blackberry is a cluster of very small drupes, each containing a tiny stone. The actual seeds, often called kernels, are inside the stones. Apples and pears belong to a fruit type called 'pomes'. These are fruits with a fleshy outer layer and a paper like core that contains a number of seeds. Many of the juicy fruits that we eat are specially cultivated and much larger than their wild ancestors as a result of special breeding. Many of what we call vegetables are actually fruits, including marrows and runner beans.

Most plants have developed ways of scattering their seeds so that they do not all fall under the parent plant. The hooked burs of the burdock contain many small fruits, which gradually fall out as the burs are carried away by animals.

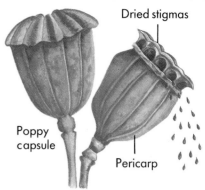

▲ The seeds of the poppy develop in the poppy's dry fruits, or capsules.

▼ Some fruits, including pea pods, explode when they are ripe and throw out their seeds. The fruits of some waterside plants float away on the water, but most plants use animals or the wind to scatter their seeds. Ashkeys spiral to the ground and can be blown some way from their parent tree. Other fruits rely on being eaten by animals and having their seeds deposited far from the parent plant.

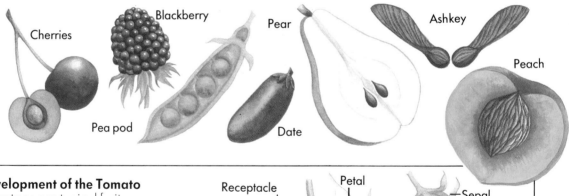

Development of the Tomato

Tomatoes are typical fruits of the type known as berries. This type also includes oranges, lemons, bananas, melons and grapes, but only a very few of the fruits with 'berry' in their names. Tomatoes develop from clusters of small yellow flowers. After the flowers are pollinated (usually by insects) the ovule begins to swell as the seeds develop inside the fleshy pericarp. The whole process takes 40 to 75 days.

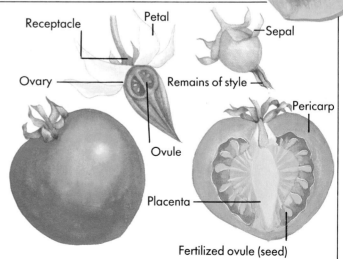

Ovary The hollow structure near the base of a flower where the seeds of the fruit are held.
Pericarp The three layers of the wall of an ovary of a mature fruit.
Simple fruit This type of fruit develops from a single ovary.
Compound fruit This type of fruit develops from two or more ovaries.
Receptacle The top of the stalk of a flower.

▼ *The acorn is a single-seeded dry fruit. The germinating seed forces its way through the fruit wall. The marrow is a berry — a juicy fruit containing several seeds.*

Acorn

Marrow

▲ *The coco de mer is a large kind of coconut. It is dropped from its parent palm on to the shore and is light enough to float to different islands.*

▼ *Fruits develop in the ovaries of the plant's flower. The apple, like the pear, is a type of fruit called a pome.*

SEE FOR YOURSELF
Cut an apple in half and look at its structure. Apples have a fleshy outer layer and a paper-like core which encloses 2 or more seeds. Compare the apple with other fruits, such as a peach, which is a fleshy fruit with a hard inner stone that encloses a single seed.

Apple

Stigma

Stamen

Style

Sepal

Ovary wall

Receptacle

Remains of stamens and sepals

▼ *Bananas are odd-shaped berries. Wild bananas have seeds, but the cultivated ones we eat, which are hybrids, seldom have seeds because they are infertile.*

Banana

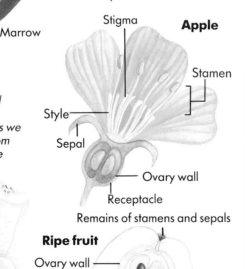

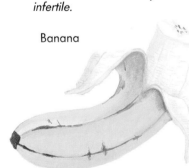

Ripe fruit

Ovary wall

Ovule

Receptacle

See also BOTANY; BREEDING; CELL DIVISION; EGGS; FERTILIZATION; GROWTH; HYBRID; POLLEN AND POLLINATION; REPRODUCTION; SEEDS.

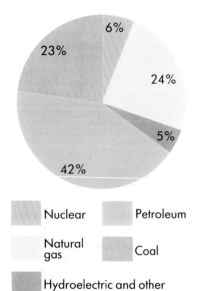

6%

23%

24%

5%

42%

Nuclear

Petroleum

Natural gas

Coal

Hydroelectric and other

▲ *This chart shows that petroleum is now the leading source of energy in the United States. Coal was once the main source of energy.*

▶ *Since the 1970s, the shortage of some fuels has led to world exploitation of other sources of energy. Nuclear power is one such example.*

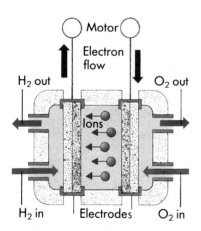

Motor

Electron flow

H_2 out O_2 out

Ions

H_2 in   Electrodes O_2 in

▲ *Hydrogen and oxygen are pumped into a cell where they are made to react by a catalyst in the electrodes. This reaction produces electricity, with water as a by-product.*

Fuel

A fuel is a material that has ENERGY stored inside it. When a fuel is burned, the energy is released as HEAT and it can be used to power MACHINES and ENGINES. The most widely used fuels are materials that were living organisms millions of years ago; these fuels are called FOSSIL FUELS. Coal, oil and gas were all formed from layers of decomposing organisms which gradually became covered in layers of rocks and other deposits. The energy they absorbed from the Sun can be released by burning them. The most convenient form of energy is ELECTRICITY, but it is also a very inefficient use of fossil fuel because when electricity is made in power stations, over two-thirds of the energy in the coal or oil is lost as heat to the atmosphere. Nuclear reactors use a different

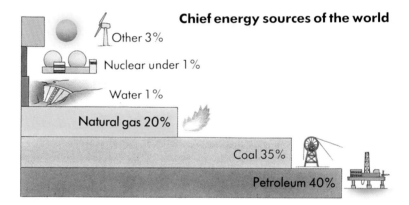

Chief energy sources of the world

Other 3%

Nuclear under 1%

Water 1%

Natural gas 20%

Coal 35%

Petroleum 40%

source of energy. They are fuelled by unstable materials such as URANIUM and PLUTONIUM. These ATOMS continually split apart, releasing large amounts of energy. This is used to generate steam to drive steam turbine power generators to produce electricity.

Fuel cell

A fuel cell is a device that generates ELECTRICITY by converting the chemical ENERGY stored in a FUEL directly into electrical energy. This is a very efficient form of energy conversion. Fuel cells are used to generate electricity on board manned spacecraft. Hydrogen fuel and oxygen are combined chemically in the fuel cell to produce electricity and, as a by-product, water. The fuel cell provides all the water the crew needs during a mission for drinking, washing and re-hydrating dehydrated (dried) food.

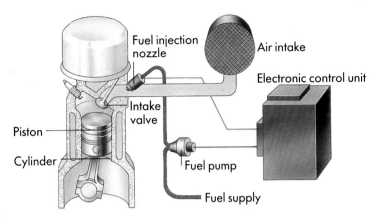

Fuel injection nozzle

Air intake

Electronic control unit

Intake valve

Piston

Cylinder

Fuel pump

Fuel supply

◀ *In a fuel injection system, fuel is sprayed into a chamber where it is mixed with air. A valve opens and admits the mixture to the cylinder. This process is computer-controlled in very modern cars.*

Fuel injection

Fuel injection is a way of feeding FUEL to an INTERNAL COMBUSTION ENGINE by pumping it into the ENGINE'S cylinders instead of sucking it in by the action of the pistons. In a petrol engine without fuel injection, a valve is opened to a cylinder and the piston moves down inside the cylinder. A spray of fuel supplied by the carburettor is sucked into the cylinder. Fuel injection is more efficient than a carburettor because it distributes fuel more evenly to all the cylinders. In DIESEL ENGINES fuel injectors are also used to spray fuel into the cylinders. Engines with no pistons, such as gas turbines, cannot operate without a fuel injection system.

Fuse

A fuse is a device for protecting electric CIRCUITS and the people who use them. Every circuit needs an electric current to operate. If the circuit or its ELECTRICITY supply develop a fault, too much current may flow and damage the circuit or cause a fire. A fuse is placed in the electrical supply line to prevent this. The most commonly used type of fuse is a length of thin wire inside a glass tube between two metal end-caps. When a circuit operates correctly, the fuse allows current to pass through. If the current rises, the fuse-wire heats up and melts, or 'blows', breaking the circuit. Thicker fuse wire allows a higher current to flow before it breaks. Fuses are available with different current 'ratings'. Some homes are fitted with CIRCUIT BREAKERS instead of fuses. These can be reset like a switch after a current overload.

Fusion, nuclear *See* Nuclear physics

SEE FOR YOURSELF
Make a circuit that includes a 4.5-volt battery, a 3.5-volt bulb and a switch. Using sticky tape, attach a strand of fine steel wool to the circuit. Close the switch. After a few seconds the wire breaks and the bulb goes out. The steel wool does not conduct electricity as easily as the thicker wires in the circuit, so like a fuse it gets hot and breaks.

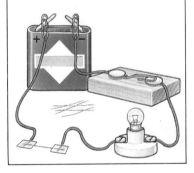

The wire in the bottom fuse has been melted by the heat of too large a current. It is important to fit the correct fuse to each appliance. A lamp needs a fuse rated at **3 amps**; a television, hair dryer or refrigerator needs **5 amps**; and electric fires and washing machines need **13 amps**. Cookers need special wiring fused at **30 amps**.

▶ *Spiral galaxies contain old stars but also large numbers of young stars, gas and dust.*

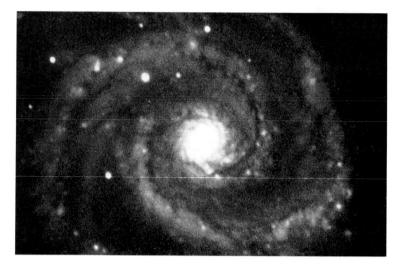

▼ *Galaxies are different shapes. The Milky Way is a spiral galaxy, with arms wrapped around its nucleus or centre. It takes about 225 million years to spin round once. Another type of spiral galaxy is known as a barred-spiral galaxy. Elliptical galaxies are like spirals that have lost their arms, while some galaxies are irregular with no particular shape.*

Irregular galaxy

Elliptical galaxy

Galaxy

Stars occur in galaxies, independent 'star cities' which formed soon after the UNIVERSE came into existence about 15,000 million years ago. To begin with, the galaxies were just huge clouds of gas, mainly HYDROGEN. Then GRAVITY pulled the gas together into separate clouds that heated up and began to shine as STARS.

The stars that first formed have now cooled and dimmed, but new stars are still being born inside most galaxies. In our own galaxy, the Milky Way, there are huge clouds of hydrogen mixed with specks of solid matter, such as carbon, which may one day form stars.

Galaxies range from 'dwarfs', with perhaps a million stars, to 'supergiants', with perhaps a million million. The Milky Way has about 100,000 million stars.

Galaxies occur in clusters. There are about 30 in the Milky Way's cluster, but some clusters contain hundreds. These clusters, in turn, may belong to 'superclusters'. The clusters of galaxies are flying apart from each other as the Universe expands from the BIG BANG.

Spiral galaxy

Barred spiral galaxy

Galileo Galilei

Galileo Galilei (1564–1642), who lived in Italy, is remembered as the first person to turn a TELESCOPE to the sky and make important astronomical discoveries. He observed craters on the MOON, the bright satellites of JUPITER, SUNSPOTS and other things.

He made himself unpopular, because he lived at a time when belief about the world and the UNIVERSE was based on the Bible and on ARISTOTLE's teachings of 2000 years earlier. For example, Aristotle had said that a heavy weight fell more quickly than a light one, but Galileo showed that they both fell at the same speed. The Bible said that everything moves around the Earth, but Galileo's observations showed that the Earth moves round the Sun. He was imprisoned, and ended his life near Florence under 'house arrest'.

▲ Galileo was one of the first people to perform experiments in order to find things out.

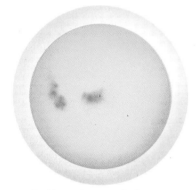

▶ Galileo observed objects circling Jupiter. The four largest moons of Jupiter are known as the Galilean Satellites.

◀ Spots on the Sun as Galileo might have seen them. He did not observe the Sun directly to protect his eyes.

▲ Galileo built several telescopes. He built the first in 1609. With his telescopes Galileo saw that the Moon was not smooth and perfect as generally believed, but that it was covered with mountains and craters. Galileo also discovered that a pendulum could be used to measure time. He found this out by watching a hanging lamp swinging in Pisa Cathedral. He realized that it took exactly the same time for each swing, whether the swings were large or small.

Galvani, Luigi *See* Galvanometer

Galvanizing

Galvanizing is an industrial process for rust-proofing IRON AND STEEL by covering the metal with a thin layer of ZINC. It can be done in two ways: dipping and electrodeposition. In dipping, the metal is cleaned by dipping it in acid and then dipped into a bath of molten zinc. When it is taken out, it is covered by a thin layer of zinc. Alternatively, iron and steel can be galvanized by an electrical method. Two electrodes, a positive anode and a negative cathode, are dipped into a SOLUTION, or electrolyte, containing zinc, for example, zinc sulphate. The

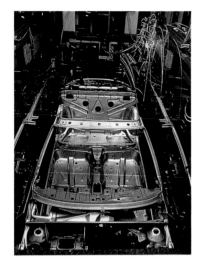

▲ *The steel shell of a car is galvanized, coated with a layer of zinc alloy, which protects it from corrosion.*

object to be galvanized is connected to the cathode. When the current flows, zinc ions from the solution are deposited over the cathode and the object connected to it. This is called ELECTROLYSIS. The thickness of the zinc coating depends on the time spent in the electrolyte.

Galvanometer

A galvanometer is a device for measuring the electric current flowing in a CIRCUIT. It uses Michael FARADAY's discovery that a wire carrying a current in a magnetic field experiences a FORCE. The current which is to be measured is passed through a coil of fine wire, which is pivoted between the poles of a magnet. When the current passes through the coil, the coil becomes a magnet and tries to turn itself into line with the poles of the magnet. Springs attached to the coil hold it steady. A pointer or mirror is attached to the coil and enables the current

Luigi Galvani (1737–1798)
Galvani was an Italian scientist. He is known for his experiments showing the effects of electricity on living tissue, particularly on muscles. He discovered that touching the nerves in a dead frog's leg with a pair of scissors during a thunderstorm caused the muscles to twitch. Galvani believed that he had discovered a new type of electricity, animal electricity, but Alessandro Volta showed that this was not the case. Galvani's name lives on in the 'galvanometer' and in the word 'galvanized', which means stimultated as if by electricity.

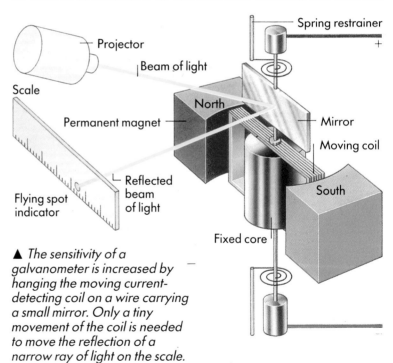

▲ *The sensitivity of a galvanometer is increased by hanging the moving current-detecting coil on a wire carrying a small mirror. Only a tiny movement of the coil is needed to move the reflection of a narrow ray of light on the scale.*

flowing to be read from a scale. The electrical RESISTANCE of the galvanometer is very small so that it does not affect the current.

Galvanometers are now being replaced by more accurate DIGITAL instruments.

Gamma rays *See* Radioactivity

Gas

Gas is one of the three STATES OF MATTER, the others being SOLID and LIQUID. The tiny MOLECULES that make up matter are in constant motion. In a gas, the molecules are more loosely held together than they are in a solid or liquid. In a gas, they can move around freely. Thus, a gas will always expand to fill its container. It takes its shape from its container but does not take up a definite amount of space (that is, it has no fixed volume). Released from its container, it will go on expanding. The molecules in a gas move rapidly and randomly and bump into each other and into the inside of the container exerting PRESSURE on it.

If the same amount of gas is put into a container half

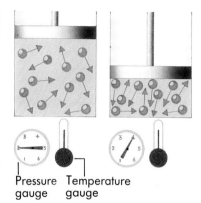

Pressure Temperature
gauge   gauge

▲ *Gas pressure doubles if its volume is halved and its temperature remains constant.*

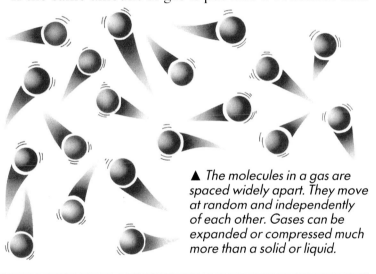

▲ *The molecules in a gas are spaced widely apart. They move at random and independently of each other. Gases can be expanded or compressed much more than a solid or liquid.*

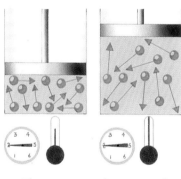

▲ *The pressure of gas stays the same if the temperature and the volume double. The rise in temperature makes the molecules move faster but in more space.*

Gay-Lussac was a French chemist. In 1802, working independently, he repeated the discovery that another chemist, Jacques Charles, had already made about the constant expansion of gases with each degree rise in temperature. Gay-Lussac later showed that, when gaseous elements combine to form compounds, they do so in proportions by volume that can be expressed as simple whole numbers. For example, forming water, two parts by volume of hydrogen combine with one part by volume of oxygen.

Joseph Louis Gay-Lussac (1778–1850)

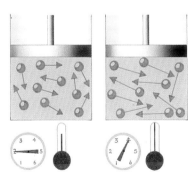

▲ *The pressure of gas doubles if the volume remains the same and the temperature doubles. The rise in temperature causes the molecules to move faster in the same space.*

279

**Jacques Charles
(1746–1823)**
Charles was a French chemist who was also a teacher and a minor government official. Charles is best known for stating the law that every gas expands by the same amount for a rise in temperature of one degree. This means that the volume of a fixed amount of gas is directly proportional to the temperature if the pressure remains constant. Charles did not publish his research and it was later duplicated by Gay-Lussac. He was also interested in ballooning and suggested balloons could be filled with the very light hydrogen gas.

the size, the pressure of the gas doubles, as long as the TEMPERATURE remains unchanged. If, however, a gas is heated, the molecules will move faster and further apart. If the gas is prevented from expanding by its container, its pressure on the container will increase. If a gas is cooled enough, it will become a liquid. If gases are squeezed during cooling, they become liquid at a temperature above their BOILING POINT.
See also NATURAL GAS.

Gas turbine

A gas turbine is a type of INTERNAL COMBUSTION ENGINE used by many aircraft and ships, and some tanks. It was invented in the 1940s during World War II (1939–1945) by the British engineer, Frank Whittle. It works by burning fuel in compressed air like a piston engine, but it has no pistons. Beyond a certain upper speed limit, piston engines risk shaking themselves apart. In a gas turbine, the expanding COMBUSTION gases are used to drive a TURBINE. This can power the compressor that sucks air into the engine and compress it before leaving the engine as a jet of hot gas. This gives the engine its popular name, the turbojet or jet engine. In the turboprop engine, the turbine drives a propeller. In a turboshaft engine, the

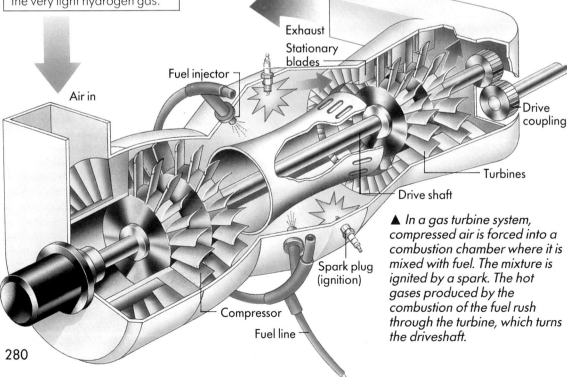

Air in · Fuel injector · Exhaust · Stationary blades · Drive coupling · Turbines · Drive shaft · Spark plug (ignition) · Compressor · Fuel line

▲ *In a gas turbine system, compressed air is forced into a combustion chamber where it is mixed with fuel. The mixture is ignited by a spark. The hot gases produced by the combustion of the fuel rush through the turbine, which turns the driveshaft.*

turbine drives a shaft that may power a tank's tracks or a helicopter's rotors.

See also JET PROPULSION.

Gasoline *See* Petroleum

Gay-Lussac, Joseph Louis *See* Gas

Gears

Gears are toothed wheels used in MACHINES to make one shaft turn another. The first wheel is called the driver and the second, the follower. Driver and follower rotate in opposite directions. If driver and follower are the same size, both shafts rotate at the same speed. Often one shaft is required to rotate more slowly or more quickly than the engine driving it. This can be achieved using gear wheels of different sizes. If a shaft fitted with a small driver drives a larger follower, the shaft from the follower rotates more slowly than the driver shaft. The opposite is also true. If the shafts need to rotate in the same direction, a third gear called an idler can be inserted between the driver and follower. Gears are also used to change the direction of movement of a shaft.

A car engine has gears to enable it to travel at a range of speeds. The engine is only connected directly to the

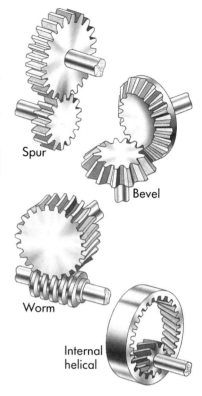

Spur

Bevel

Worm

Internal helical

▲ *These are some common types of gears. Gear teeth are specially constructed to fit smoothly, reducing wear and tear, vibration and noise.*

SEE FOR YOURSELF
Make a frame out of wood or use a cardboard box. Take 2 corks and stick 6 evenly spaced pins into each of them to make gears. Push fine knitting-needles through each of the corks. Insert the ends of the knitting-needles into pieces of stiff card to hold them in place. Fix a handle to one end of the horizontal knitting-needle and a small shape to the top of the vertical knitting-needle. Make sure the pins on each of the gears overlap. By turning the handle on the horizontal shaft anti-clockwise, the vertical shaft is caused to turn anticlockwise.

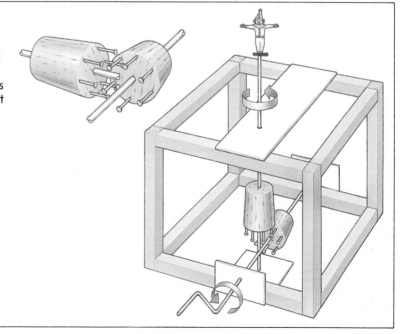

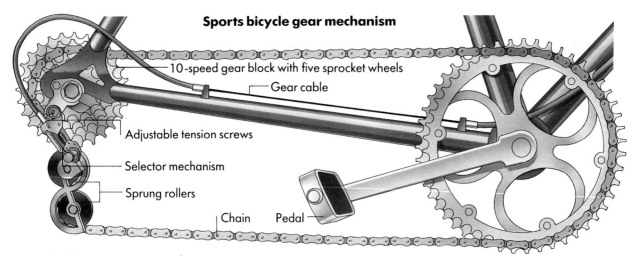

Sports bicycle gear mechanism

10-speed gear block with five sprocket wheels

Gear cable

Adjustable tension screws

Selector mechanism

Sprung rollers

Chain   Pedal

▲ *The gear system used on a racing bicycle. The selector moves the chain to a different sprocket wheel.*

▼ *Radiation entering a Geiger counter tube causes gas atoms inside it to ionize. This releases electrons which create electric pulses that are counted by a meter.*

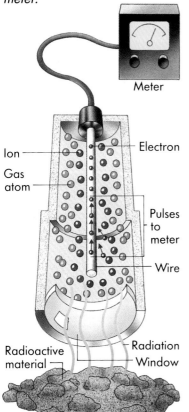

Meter

Ion

Gas atom

Electron

Pulses to meter

Wire

Radioactive material

Radiation

Window

road wheels in the highest gear. In other gears, the engine's output shaft is spinning faster than the wheels.

Geiger counter

A Geiger counter is an instrument designed to detect and measure RADIOACTIVITY. It was invented in 1908 by the German scientist, Hans Geiger, after whom it is named. It consists of a sealed tube with one fine wire electrode running down the middle. The tube itself is the other electrode. The tube, filled with a GAS such as argon, is charged to a very high voltage, perhaps 1000 volts. If an atomic particle enters the tube, it 'ionizes' the gas, that is, it splits the electrically neutral gas into positively charged IONS and negatively charged ELECTRONS. The positive ions rush to one electrode and the electrons to the other electrode. This triggers a momentary electric current from one electrode to the other. The number of atomic particles detected by the counter can be displayed on a scale or as a series of audible clicks.

Gemstones *See* Minerals

Generator, electric

An electric generator is a machine which converts mechanical motion into an electrical current. Generators work by using the principle of electromagnetic INDUCTION discovered by FARADAY. Coils of wire are mounted so that they can be spun around in a magnetic field. This means that the magnetic field is pointing first one way through the coils, then the other; the changing magnetic

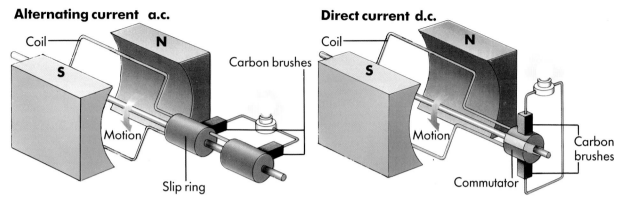

Alternating current a.c.

Coil

N

S

Motion

Carbon brushes

Slip ring

Direct current d.c.

Coil

N

S

Motion

Carbon brushes

Commutator

field produces a current around the coil. This type of generator is called an *alternator* because the increase and decrease of the magnetic field produces an alternating current. To generate a direct current (always in the same direction), the coil has to be connected to a *commutator*. The commutator makes the current flow continuously in one direction.

Mechanical ENERGY is needed to turn the coil to create electrical energy. The ELECTRICITY we use is generated by power stations; usually the energy from burning coal or from a nuclear reaction is used to make steam, which drives a TURBINE to produce the mechanical energy to turn the generator coils around.

▲ *These are two simple generators, an alternating current (a.c.) and a direct current (d.c.) generator. Inside each type of generator is a wire coil, which is held between the two poles of a magnet. When the wire coil turns in the magnetic field, electricity is produced in the wire. The magnetic force makes electrons in the wire coil move, generating an electric current. An a.c. generator is joined to the rest of the circuit by a slip ring and carbon brushes. The d.c. generator has a device, called a commutator, for reversing or altering the electric current. This is so that the current always flows the same way instead of alternating (flowing in one direction and then the other).*

Direct current (d.c.) generator

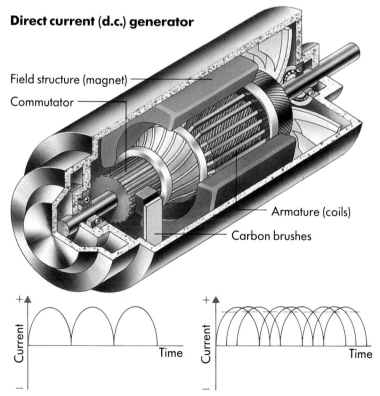

Field structure (magnet)

Commutator

Armature (coils)

Carbon brushes

Current / Time

Current / Time

◄ *The output values of a direct current generator, with a single coil, vary as the electromotive force changes direction. Because of this, commercial generators have several coils wound around the armature so that an almost constant amount of electricity can be produced. Each coil is connected to its own segment at the commutator.*

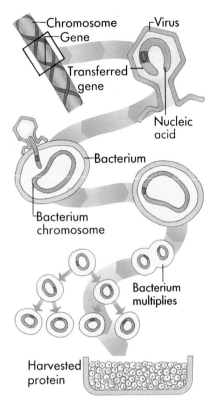

Chromosome
Gene
Virus
Transferred gene
Nucleic acid
Bacterium
Bacterium chromosome
Bacterium multiplies
Harvested protein

▲ *A protein-producing gene, such as that for insulin, is cut from human DNA. This is then spliced into the nucleic acid of a virus. The virus injects the nucleic acid into a bacterium. The gene becomes part of the bacterium's chromosome. This bacterium can now make insulin which it could not make before. Many bacteria are grown together in a fermenter. The insulin they produce is separated and purified for use in treating diabetics.*

▶ *These false-coloured plasmids of bacterial DNA come from the bacterium Escherichia coli. 'Foreign' DNA is joined to the plasmid and the new plasmid is then put into an Escherichia coli bacterium where it makes copies of the genetic information carried by the transplanted 'foreign' DNA.*

Genetic engineering

Genetic engineering is a form of BIOTECHNOLOGY in which the genes of an organism are deliberately altered in order to change its characteristics. A simple example is the development of genetically-engineered grapefruit. The genes of an ordinary grapefruit were changed by exposing them to radiation, causing changes or MUTATIONS, which resulted in pink-fleshed grapefruit which taste sweeter than normal. In this case the results depended largely upon luck, but deliberate genetic engineering can make very dramatic changes. For example, genes controlling the production of insulin in humans or animals can be inserted into a bacterium which is easily grown and harvested, so the 'human' insulin produced can be used to treat people with diabetes. Bacteria and yeasts are usually used for this type of genetic engineering because their genetic structure is well known and they can be easily grown in the laboratory by FERMENTATION.

Food crops are also produced by genetic engineering, and special types are being developed which resist DISEASE, and grow faster than normal crops.
See also BREEDING; CHROMOSOMES AND GENES.

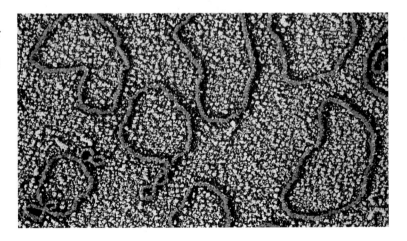

Geography

Geography was originally the study of the surface of the EARTH. Nowadays, geography has been broadened to cover the study of the origins, formation and landforms of the Earth and the distribution of life upon it. Geography is sometimes divided into regional geography and systematic geography. *See* pages 286 and 287.

GENETICS

Genetics is based upon the scientific study of heredity. For centuries, farmers have carefully selected strains of livestock and crops and bred from them in order to improve their stock, to make them grow faster, or to develop some special characteristic. This was not done on a scientific basis, and it was often a matter of luck if the resulting animal or plant was better than its parents. The Austrian monk Gregor Mendel, experimenting with cross-breeding peas, was the first to deduce that some hereditary material came from both parents, and he laid down the simple rules that govern heredity in these plants. He published this information in 1866, but it was overlooked until 1900, when the science of genetics was just beginning. Since then, genetics has progressed very rapidly, with scientists now able to understand much of the workings of the genetic material and to breed new strains of organisms with ease. This is the positive side of genetics, which has led to the development of crops yielding much more grain than was ever possible before, and sheep which routinely produce twins, and so double the farmers' output of lambs. Working at the microscopic level, the science of genetics is used to breed microorganisms which in turn will make useful substances such as protein and antibiotics. On the negative side, some people are worried that genetics could be misused, for example, to produce new diseases for biological warfare. Similarly, there are fears that new organisms produced by genetic engineering could escape into the environment and cause harm.

Barbara McClintock (1902–1992)
In 1983 McLintock won the Nobel Prize for Physiology and Medicine for her discovery that some genes can change position on the chromosomes. Earlier, she had shown that when eggs or sperm are produced the chromosomes can break apart and join up again in different ways, allowing different combinations of genes in the offspring.

▼ Organisms have pairs of chromosomes that carry two genes for the same character. Often one is dominant and always shows its effects. Sometimes the two genes mix their effects as, for example, when a black female cat and a ginger male cat have kittens. Some will be tortoiseshell.

▲ This flower has a 'jumping gene', which has changed the flower colour to purple. The gene that controls the colour of the flower is unstable and can move around. When this happens the colour of the flower is changed.

Hemophilia
The hereditary disease hemophilia prevents blood from clotting normally. Hemophilia is caused by a defective gene carried on the X chromosome, one of the two sex chromosomes. A male who inherits the defective gene suffers from the disease as he has only one X chromosome. A female who inherits the defective gene does not normally suffer from the disease because she has two X chromosomes and the hemophilia gene only shows effect when there is no normal blood clot gene present, however, she may pass it on to her children.

See also BIOTECHNOLOGY; BREEDING; CELL DIVISION; CHROMOSOMES AND GENES; GENETIC ENGINEERING; HEREDITY; MICROORGANISMS.

GEOGRAPHY

Geography has its origins in the Greeks' attempts to describe the surface of the Earth on which they lived. Eratosthenes realized that the Earth was round in the 3rd century BC and 500 years later Ptolemy produced a map of the Earth which was used for centuries.

Modern geography is concerned with those aspects of the Earth's surface which could be described as the habitat occupied by the human species. It has many branches, some of which border other sciences very closely. As its name suggests, regional geography examines, on a regional basis, the ways in which the local people interact with the environment of the area in which they live. In its widest sense, systematic geography may include climatology (the study of weather and the climate), cartography (the study of maps and map projections), oceanography (the study of the seas and oceans), and even human geography and biogeography which deal with the distribution of people and their industries and systems of communications, as well as with the distribution of plants and animals.

Physical geography, which may also be called geomorphology, concentrates on the origins and formation of the landforms themselves, and often overlaps with aspects of geology, especially with regard to the processes of erosion and weathering or glaciation, for example. The study of soils was also once lumped together with geography but, nowadays, it is generally regarded as a separate discipline, called soil science. And human geography, of course, also overlaps the social sciences. Today, geographers are heavily involved with the actual planning of the cities, towns, villages and countryside in which we all live and work.

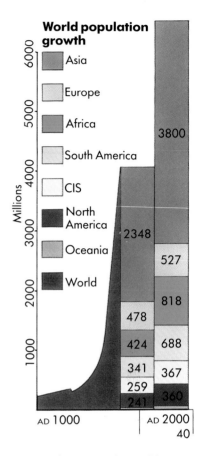

World population growth

- Asia
- Europe
- Africa
- South America
- CIS
- North America
- Oceania
- World

▲ Since the 1800s, the world population has grown from 1000 million to over 5000 million. It is expected to double in the next 40 years.

SEE FOR YOURSELF
Go to the top of a small hill and look about you. If possible get a map of the area and see if you can identify the main features of the landscape on the map. Look for churches, the pattern of roads, railways and rivers, woods, variations in land form and other dominant features.

Earth Facts
Highest mountain Mount Everest (summit 8848 m) on the borders of Tibet and Nepal in Asia.
Deepest ocean Marianas Trench in the Pacific Ocean (11,034 m).
Longest river River Nile in Africa (6670 km).
Largest land mass If Europe and Asia are taken together their area is 53,698,000 km².
Largest island Greenland (area 2,175,000 km²).
Largest lake Caspian Sea in Commonwealth of Independent States (area 360,700 km²).

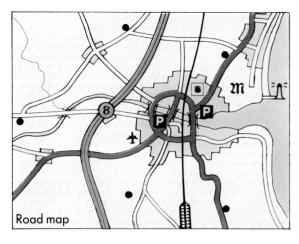

Road map

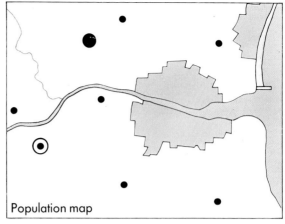

Population map

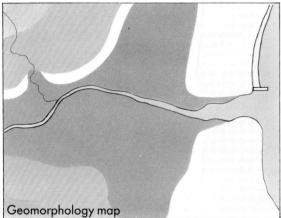

Geomorphology map

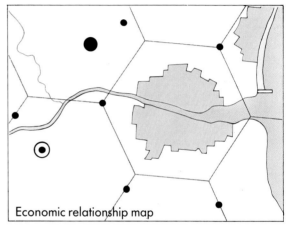

Economic relationship map

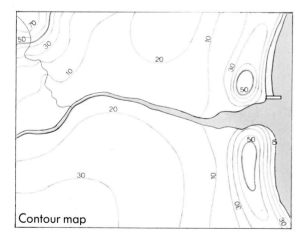

Contour map

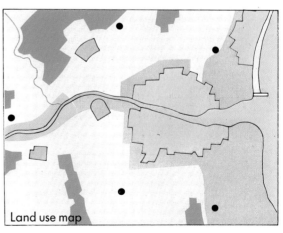

Land use map

▲ Different kinds of maps are used by geographers to give different kinds of information about our physical environment and aspects of human activity. They often present information in a simplified form. Symbols are used to represent features, such as railway stations, airports, main roads and their junctions, bridges etc. Population maps show settlement sizes and distribution. Geomorphological maps show landforms and how they are made up. Economic maps show the environmental and human factors that affect the development and growth of a region. Contour maps are made up of lines (contours) that join points of equal height which show the physical features on the land. Land use maps show the location of housing, farmland, woodland and other vegetation.

See also CLIMATE; COMMUNICATIONS; EARTH; ENVIRONMENT; GEOLOGY; LANDFORMS; MAP; MAP PROJECTION; SOIL; STATISTICS; WEATHER.

GEOLOGY

Geology is the study of the Earth, its history as a planet, its composition, structure and the changes it undergoes, especially as reflected in the rocks of which it is made. The study of the Moon in this way is called lunar geology.

Like so many sciences today, geology is usually divided into separate branches and it overlaps with other disciplines, such as geography. Geologists study: fossils and ancient life forms (paleontology); the chemistry and physics of the Earth (geochemistry and geophysics); the composition and structure of rocks (petrology); the minerals which compose rocks (mineralogy); the layers or strata in which sedimentary rocks are deposited that reflect the geological history of the Earth (stratigraphy). Much of the pioneering work was carried out in the 19th century by workers such as Lyell, Murchison, Smith, Sedgewick and Geikie, Buckland and others. Some were amateurs, but they made important contributions by painstaking studies of cliff sections and quarries.

Era	Period	Epoch	Millions of years ago
CENOZOIC	Quaternary	Recent	
			0.01
		Pleistocene	
			2
	Tertiary	Pliocene	
			5
		Miocene	
			25
		Oligocene	
			35
		Eocene	
			60
		Paleocene	
			65
MESOZOIC	Cretaceous		
			145
	Jurassic		
			210
	Triassic		
			245
PALEOZOIC	Permian		
			285
	Carboniferous		
			360
	Devonian		
			410
	Silurian		
			440
	Ordovician		
			505
	Cambrian		
			570

Precambrian.
Time stretches back to the formation of the Earth 4600 million years ago

▲ Radioactive elements scattered through rocks have made it possible to determine their ages. Using this and the method of estimating the relative ages of rocks from the probable dates when they were formed, a general geological time scale has been worked out.

SEE FOR YOURSELF
Next time you visit a beach or an old quarry, see whether you can find different layers of rock in the cliffs. These may include sandstone, a streaky sandy colour; clay, a dark reddish brown and limestone, which is white.

Charles Lyell (1797–1875)
Lyell was a British scientist. He is often called the father of modern geology. In his book *Principles of Geology*, published between 1830 and 1833, he showed that the Earth has changed slowly and gradually through the ages by means of processes that are still going on. He was one of the first scientists to accept modern theories about the Ice Age and evolution.

See also FOSSILS; IGNEOUS ROCKS; METAMORPHIC ROCKS; MINERALS; PALEONTOLOGY; PLATE TECTONICS; ROCKS; SEDIMENTARY ROCKS.

Geomagnetism

Geomagnetism is the name given to the MAGNETISM of the EARTH. Like a planet-sized bar magnet, the Earth's magnetic field is oriented to give a magnetic North Pole and a magnetic South Pole. Magnetic North and South do not coincide exactly with the geographical poles and, because the Earth's magnetic field slowly changes (and even reverses over very long periods), the difference between magnetic and geographic north varies with time. A consequence of this is that MAPS must be adjusted to take account of such variations. It is thought that the Earth's magnetic field results from currents set up in the liquid outer core of the planet as it rotates.

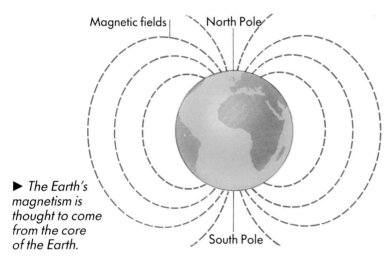

▶ *The Earth's magnetism is thought to come from the core of the Earth.*

Geometry

Geometry is the branch of MATHEMATICS that tells us about points, lines, curves and surfaces, how they relate to each other, and how we measure them. It involves the study of plane (flat) figures, such as the square, triangle and circle, and solid, three-dimensional figures, such as the cube, pyramid and sphere. *Geometry* means 'measurement of the Earth', and the first practical uses of it concerned the MEASUREMENT of land areas, such as fields. Today architects, builders, carpenters, civil engineers, artists, photographers and jewellers rely on a knowledge of geometry to do their work. The navigation of aircraft and ships relies on the principles of geometry to calculate the craft's position in air or sea.

Geometry accepts that certain definitions and statements (called axioms) are true and uses them to discover

Wilhelm Weber (1804–1891)
Weber was a German physicist known for his work on geomagnetism. He researched wave motion in 1824 and the mechanics of walking in 1833. The weber unit of magnetic flux (Wb) is named after him. A strong magnetic field may have a strength of two or more webers per square metre.

Pythagoras (c. 560–480BC)
Pythagoras was an ancient Greek philosopher and mathematician. He taught the importance of numbers, notably in music. His most famous work was in geometry. His famous Pythagorean Theorem states that in a right-angled triangle, the square on the hypotenuse (the side opposite the right angle) equals the sum of the squares on the other two sides.

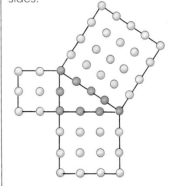

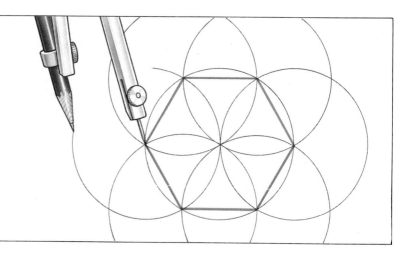

and prove or disprove other statements called theorems. *See also* ALGEBRA; ARITHMETIC; POLYGON; SYMMETRY.

Geostationary orbit

An artificial SATELLITE near the EARTH orbits faster than one far away. A satellite 35,900 km above the Earth's surface takes 24 hours to orbit once. Therefore it is always above the same point on the Earth's surface as our planet rotates. Geostationary orbit can also be called 'geosynchronous' orbit (in time with the Earth).

Some kinds of radio waves are reflected around the Earth by the IONOSPHERE high in the ATMOSPHERE. But TELEVISION signals pass right through it and so geostationary satellites are used to transmit signals over long distances, for example, one over the Atlantic allows signals to pass between America and Europe.

35,900 km

24 hours

▲ *Geostationary satellites orbit the Earth once every 24 hours in the same time it takes the Earth to spin once on its axis, so that they remain in the same spot above the Earth's surface. They are used to receive telephone and television signals and re-transmit them over long distances.*

Geothermal energy

Geothermal ENERGY is obtained by tapping the HEAT generated within the EARTH. The Earth's temperature rises with depth. Heat generated beneath the Earth's crust is distributed through the crust by volcanic and other igneous processes. If GROUNDWATER seeping deep within the crust should become trapped, it may be heated to form steam. By drilling a well, it is possible to harness this steam to drive electric GENERATORS.

Sometimes, water may not be hot enough to become steam but it is possible to use the hot water for domestic heating or in agriculture and market gardening.

Geothermal energy is one of the kinds of 'alternative

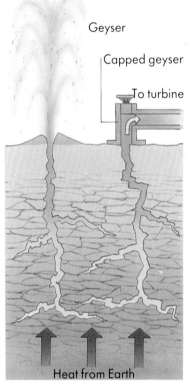

▲ *Geothermal power comes from water heated under the Earth's surface.*

▼ *Cold water seeps deep below ground until it reaches hot rocks. The water heats up, until some of it expands into steam, forcing out the rest in a rush of boiling water. This steam can be forced through a steam turbine to create power.*

Geyser

Capped geyser

To turbine

Heat from Earth

energy'. It is clean, but no one knows the effects on the Earth's system of tapping large amounts of energy.

Gestation

Gestation is the early development, from the time of FERTILIZATION to the moment of BIRTH. Before you were born, you spent about nine months growing inside your mother's body. Among the mammals, generally, the larger the animal the longer the gestation period, although there are some exceptions. Mammalian gestation periods range from about 18 days in some mice, to about 21 months in the Indian elephant. Most other groups of animals lay EGGS, but some reptiles and amphibians, a number of fishes and some insects give birth to live young. The longest recorded gestation period is that of the Alpine salamander, which has been known to carry its babies for 38 months. Everything takes place very slowly in the cold mountain climate and the adults may only be active for three months in a year.

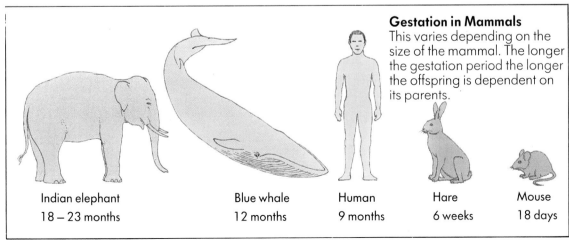

Gestation in Mammals
This varies depending on the size of the mammal. The longer the gestation period the longer the offspring is dependent on its parents.

Indian elephant	Blue whale	Human	Hare	Mouse
18 – 23 months	12 months	9 months	6 weeks	18 days

▲ *This axolotl's external gills can be clearly seen. Oxygen from the water is transferred into the blood vessels of the gills and then into the body.*

Gilbert, William *See* Magnetism

Gills

All animals need to be able to obtain OXYGEN from the environment in which they live, and at the same time they must get rid of waste CARBON DIOXIDE. Land animals do this by extracting oxygen from the air with LUNGS or some similar organ. Animals which live in the water use gills. Gills have a mass of very fine BLOOD vessels exposed to water, allowing the transfer of oxygen and carbon dioxide. Simple gills are tufts of tissue containing blood vessels, such as are seen in young tadpoles. The tufts provide a large surface area for gas transfer. In fish, these gills are protected inside the head. Water is continuously pumped through the mouth past the gills, so they are always exposed to oxygen in the water.

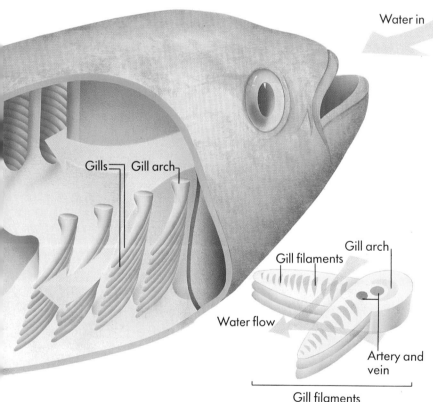

Water in

Gills Gill arch

Gill filaments

Gill arch

Water flow

Artery and vein

Gill filaments

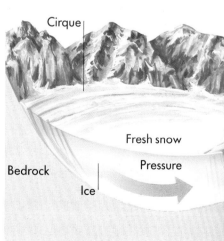

▼ *A glacier starts in a cirque, a bowl-shaped hollow near a mountain peak. The glacier picks up rocks and other debris and piles them up in ridges called moraines. The hilly ridge at the bottom of a glacier is called a terminal moraine. Glaciers move faster at the centre than at the sides. This can create huge gaps or crevasses.*

Cirque

Fresh snow

Bedrock

Pressure

Ice

▲ *Fish gills vary in form but all are designed to present the largest possible surface containing blood vessels to the water. Water enters through the* mouth and flows over the gills and out through the gill slits. Gills are made of threadlike filaments attached to a gill arch. Most fish have four pairs of gills.

◀ *The Mendenhall glacier is a valley glacier. These are long, narrow bodies of ice that fill mountain valleys.*

▼ *When a glacier melts it leaves behind roches moutonnées, which are lumps of polished rock surfaces; rounded hills, called drumlins; and narrow ridges of rock debris, called eskers. Hollows in the loose rock trap water, forming meltwater and kettle lakes. A retreating glacier may leave great semicircular ridges in front of the outwash plain.*

Glacier

A glacier is a large body of ICE which may form in a MOUNTAIN valley or in an area, such as at either of the polar regions where the volume of snow which falls in the cold season of the year is greater than the amount which melts during the warmer season. As the snow accumulates, the snow below is compressed and the spaces between the snow flakes are filled with ice. Ice is a solid material and, like most solids, it seems rigid. In fact, provided the temperature of the glacier is close to the MELTING POINT, the glacier is able to flow slowly downslope and to bend under its weight.

There are two main kinds of glaciers. The ice sheets of Antarctica which may reach thicknesses of more than 4000 m and the ice which accumulates in snowy and mountainous areas, and flows slowly down the valley.

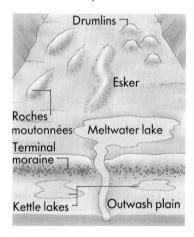

Drumlins

Esker

Roches moutonnées

Meltwater lake

Terminal moraine

Kettle lakes

Outwash plain

▼ *Rocks and other debris carried by the glacier are deposited as moraines. When glaciers meet they form a medial moraine.*

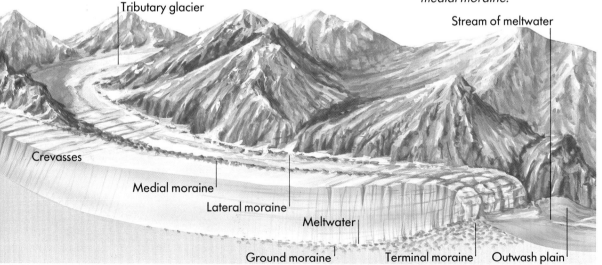

Tributary glacier

Stream of meltwater

Crevasses

Medial moraine

Lateral moraine

Meltwater

Ground moraine

Terminal moraine

Outwash plain

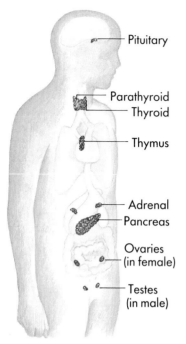

▲ *The positions of the major endocrine glands in the body.*

Pituitary
Parathyroid
Thyroid
Thymus
Adrenal
Pancreas
Ovaries (in female)
Testes (in male)

▼ *The sebaceous glands are the glands that lubricate the skin and hair.*

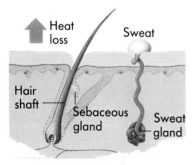

Heat loss
Sweat
Hair shaft
Sebaceous gland
Sweat gland

▶ *The glass blower dips his blow tube into molten glass. He then blows gently into the blow pipe while turning it. Turning the blow pipe prevents the glass from dropping off the end. As he blows the glass bulges out and forms a hollow bulb, which can be squeezed, stretched and cut.*

Glands

Glands are organs which produce secretions that are passed out of the gland to carry out their function elsewhere in the body. The secretions are made in specially modified CELLS which are grouped into a gland. Sometimes these secretions are carried away through a duct. Other glands pass their secretions into the BLOOD, which circulates them around the body. These are called endocrine glands. Many glands pass their secretions into the gut, where they assist in DIGESTION. The stomach, duodenum and small intestine are lined with glands which produce digestive ENZYMES. The pancreas is a large ducted gland which produces digestive enzymes, but also secretes the HORMONE insulin directly into the blood. Many other glands in the body also produce hormones. These function as chemical messengers which stimulate other organs to begin working, or inhibit their activity. The pituitary gland, situated at the base of the brain, produces hormones which control the function of other glands. It produces growth hormones which are important during childhood and ADOLESCENCE. When a gland fails to work properly there can be serious physical effects or illness. There are many glands in the SKIN, producing oily sebum to lubricate and protect the skin surface, and sweat glands which produce a watery secretion to cool the skin and get rid of waste products.

Glass

Glass is a transparent material used to make windows, containers and LENSES. It is also used in the manufacture of some electrical INSULATORS because it does not conduct ELECTRICITY. It is made mainly from silica, or sand. If lead oxide is added, the resulting sparkling glass, called lead crystal, is used to make fine drinking glasses.

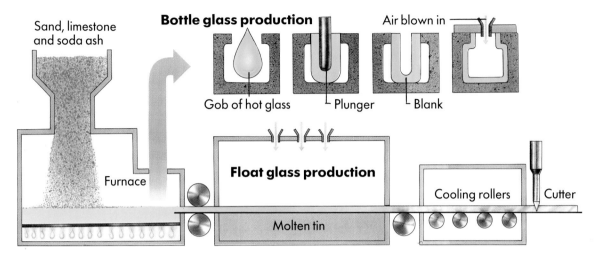

Bottle glass production

Sand, limestone and soda ash

Air blown in

Gob of hot glass — Plunger — Blank

Furnace

Float glass production

Cooling rollers — Cutter

Molten tin

Glass can be coloured by adding other metal OXIDES.

Glass is made by heating the raw materials in a furnace. They melt and combine to give a red-hot liquid which cools to form glass. While it is hot, it can be blown or cast into different shapes. Until the 1960s, window glass was made from plate glass which had to be ground flat and polished. It was replaced by float glass. Safety glass does not splinter when it breaks: toughened glass is made by rapidly cooling a sheet of glass in a jet of cold air; laminated glass consists of two sheets of glass with a layer of plastic in between. Glass fibres set in plastic resin are used to make strong lightweight structures including some vehicle bodies.

See also OPTICAL FIBRES; SILICON.

▲ *Silica, limestone and colouring ingredients are the main materials used in glass making. These are loaded into a furnace where they melt at a temperature of 1200–1400°C. Molten glass from the furnace is moulded and blown into hollow shapes or shaped into flat sheets by the float glass process. Float glass is made by letting a layer of molten glass set on top of a bath of molten tin until it is hard. The glass is then cooled and cut into lengths.*

Globular clusters

These are vast swarms of STARS, up to a hundred thousand or more, which were formed many thousands of millions of years ago. The stars in a globular cluster are RED GIANTS, much older than the SUN or SOLAR SYSTEM.

All stars are formed in clusters when a NEBULA starts to break up into separate clouds of material. But globular clusters are special, partly because they are so large, and also because the stars have not drifted apart. For example, there is now no trace of the cluster in which the Sun was born. About 100 globular clusters have been observed in our MILKY WAY galaxy. They are all very far away from us, grouped around the nucleus of the galaxy. They were probably formed soon after the galaxy, at least 10,000 million years ago, so they are among the oldest objects in the UNIVERSE.

▲ *The Hercules star cluster is one example of a globular star cluster.*

H
H−C−OH
H−C−OH
H−C−OH
H

▲ *The chemical formula of glycerol is $C_3H_5(OH)_3$. It is an alcohol but also has a structure similar to a sugar. Glycerol draws water from its surroundings which makes it a valuable moisturizing agent.*

Glycerol (Glycerine)

Glycerol is a thick, clear, odourless, colourless LIQUID with a very sweet taste. It is also known as glycerine (or glycerin) or, by its chemical name, propanetriol. Glycerol occurs in nature as an ingredient of animal and vegetable FATS. It is very useful in industry and goes into making ice cream and sweets, toothpaste, synthetic resins for paints, and coatings for paper and cellophane to make them tough and flexible. It is also an ingredient of the EXPLOSIVE nitroglycerine, which is used to make dynamite. Glycerol for commercial use is obtained as a by-product in the making of soap or is synthesized from a HYDROCARBON called propene.

Goddard, Robert Hutchings See Rockets

Gold

Gold is a metallic ELEMENT, bright yellow in colour, whose great beauty and rarity have made it a highly prized treasure and a token of riches among humans for thousands of years. Gold is a soft but heavy METAL that can be freely shaped, drawn out into thin wires, and hammered into very thin gold leaf, but is resistant to the effects of many corrosive chemicals. It is very unreactive and forms few COMPOUNDS. It can be dissolved only by a mixture of nitric and hydrochloric acids. Gold is 19.3 times as dense as water.

Major deposits of gold are found in South Africa and the CIS. The gold exists in lodes or veins (thin layers of ORE in rocks in the Earth's crust), in nuggets or grains in streams, and in sea water. Gold is extracted from its ores by various methods.

People have found many uses for gold. Gold coins have been used as money throughout history. Dentists use it for filling teeth. Pure gold is said to be 24-carat gold. Much jewellery is made of 9-carat gold, which contains 9 parts by weight of gold and 15 parts of another metal such as copper.

▶ *Gold scrap. Gold was one of the first metals used by humans. Its chemical symbol, Au, comes from the Latin word for the metal, aurum. Apart from its use in making jewellery, coins and in dentistry, the electrical contacts of microchips and other electronic devices are often plated with gold. This is because gold is a good electrical conductor and protects objects from corrosion.*

Governor

A governor is used to control the speed of an ENGINE automatically. The first governors were used on STEAM ENGINES. They consist of two or three balls attached by hinged levers to a spindle driven by the engine. As the speed increases, the balls spinning around the spindle move outwards because of the CENTRIFUGAL FORCE. A collar around the spindle attached to the balls is pushed along the spindle and operates a valve that reduces the flow of steam to the engine's cylinders. As the engine speed falls, the valve opens again.

Graft *See* Transplants

Graph

A graph is a drawing that shows the relative sizes of quantities or variables. Graphs show how values change with time or how one variable changes in relation to another. There are four main types of graph. In line graphs or curves, each value is plotted as a point on the graph. The position of each point is given by coordinates, which are the distances of the point from two lines called the x-axis (a horizontal line) and the y-axis (a vertical line that crosses the x-axis at right angles). Histograms or bar graphs show information as bars of different heights. Picture graphs use small pictures of different sizes or quantities instead of bars. Pie charts show the relation of the parts of something to the whole of it, for example, the percentages of a country's budget spent on health, education, defence, and so on.

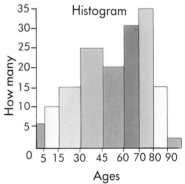

▲ *The flyball governor works by the centrifugal force of rotating weights, which move outwards against a spring. It keeps a machine running at a constant speed, normally by controlling the fuel supply.*

Spindle coupled to governor piston

Spring steel strip

Rotating weight

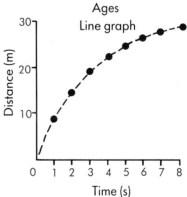

▲ *The top graph is a histogram. It is a bar graph. The bottom graph shows distance (y-axis) covered in specific periods of time (x-axis).*

Gravity on the Planets
(compared to the Earth's gravity). On a planet with a greater gravity than that of the Earth an object will appear heavier.

Mercury	0.38
Venus	0.9
Earth	1
Mars	0.38
Jupiter	2.87
Saturn	1.32
Uranus	0.93
Neptune	1.23
Pluto	0.03

Gravity

Gravity is the FORCE which pulls everything around us down towards the ground. Objects feel heavy because of the force of gravity on them. Isaac NEWTON realized that gravity is important not just for everyday objects around us, but also for the motion of PLANETS and stars. He was able to explain the orbits of all the planets known then by suggesting that gravity acts to pull together all pairs of objects with a force that depends on the amount of material or MASS in each object and on how far apart they are. The EARTH's mass is so much larger than the mass of other nearby objects that it is only the Earth's gravity that we usually notice. The gravity of more distant objects is also important; the gravitational force from the Moon moves water around in the oceans on the Earth's surface to give TIDES.

▶ In the absence of gravity, astronaut candidates experience weightlessness.

▼ Because the Moon is less massive than the Earth, the gravity it produces at its surface is only about one-sixth as strong as on Earth. Astronauts visiting the Moon are relatively only one-sixth as heavy as they would be on Earth, though their mass is the same. Therefore, they are able to leap about more easily.

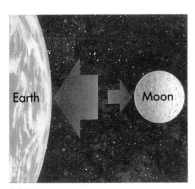

Greenhouse effect

When FOSSIL FUELS, or other FUELS, such as wood or peat, which contain carbon are burned, CARBON DIOXIDE is released into the ATMOSPHERE. Vehicles also give out, and so add, carbon dioxide to the atmosphere.

The Earth's atmosphere allows most of the Sun's rays to pass through it to heat the Earth's surface. The Earth reflects much of the heat energy back into the atmosphere, but much of this reflected radiation cannot escape because gases such as carbon dioxide absorb it. They grow warm and send heat radiation back to Earth. This is the greenhouse effect. Many scientists think that the

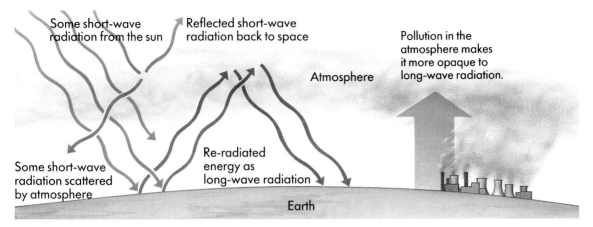

greenhouse effect may change the CLIMATE over the next 100 years or so. One consequence of so-called 'global warming' resulting from the greenhouse effect could be melting of the polar ice. This, in turn, could lead to a rise in sea level which could flood large areas of highly populated coastal land.

If carbon dioxide proves to be harmful as thought, in order to reduce carbon dioxide levels we need to reduce the amounts of carbon-rich fuels burned.

▲ *Pollution pumped into the atmosphere produces an increase in carbon dioxide, which makes it more opaque to radiation from the Earth's surface. This means that radiation is absorbed rather than passing through into space. Much of this absorbed radiation is reflected back to Earth. This may cause a gradual increase in temperature at the Earth's surface.*

Groundwater

Groundwater is water which is distributed in the ROCKS beneath the surface of the EARTH. Water is continuously being circulated between the ATMOSPHERE, the land, and the oceans, seas and rivers. Water may fall on the land as rain, snow, sleet or hail. Some of this precipitation immediately evaporates back into the atmosphere, some runs off the surface, ultimately forming rivulets, streams and then rivers, and some seeps through the soil and into the rocks beneath. Much of this groundwater is taken up by plants through their roots.

▼ *Groundwater is water that comes from beneath the surface of the Earth. The level of groundwater is called the water table. The water is collected in a layer of porous material, called an aquifer, which usually lies between layers of impermeable rocks that do not hold water. Wells are drilled down into aquifers to bring the groundwater to the surface. Groundwater also provides water for many springs.*

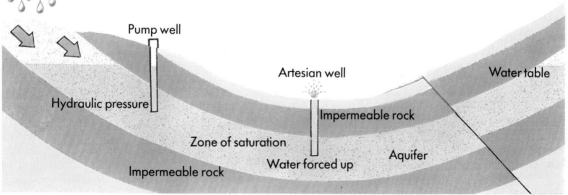

In order to reach maximum growth, an organism needs the proper nutrition at the right time. This is why adolescents usually have a large appetite, to give them enough fuel to supply energy and body-building materials for growth. Similarly, malnutrition, which often happens in time of famine, can have a serious effect on growth in children.

Growth

Growth is an increase in size of a living organism. In simple animals and plants consisting of only one CELL, growth means simply that the organism gets larger and larger, until it must reproduce by dividing itself into two parts each of which starts growing again. More complicated animals and plants made up of several cells increase in size and complexity. Usually, they begin by becoming more complex as they develop. For instance, a frog starts out as a single cell, which becomes a ball of cells, then an EMBRYO, and eventually a tadpole. Through all these stages it becomes more complex. Once it has completed its change into a tiny frog it simply grows larger, and no further changes in its structure take place. The same thing happens in humans, where development takes place in the womb, but most of the growth takes place during the 18 years or so after BIRTH.

All organisms have a maximum size. Having reached this, their cells only divide to replace those which are damaged or worn out. Growth is controlled by HORMONES which govern the way cells divide. Growth hormones control the way in which a plant shoot develops and grows upwards toward light, and the way the root grows down. Growth hormones also control the way we develop, and the rapid growth during ADOLESCENCE and the change to adulthood.

Humans grow fastest during the first six months of life. If this rate of growth was maintained, a 30-year-old man would weigh 3 billion tonnes.

SEE FOR YOURSELF
Put some potting compost, or mix together some soil and sand, in a flower pot. Make a hole about 5 cm deep and put a runner bean seed in it. Cover it up with compost or soil and water it. Place the flowerpot on a windowsill. After a few days a green shoot will appear. As the plant grows up you will need to support it with a garden cane. The plant starts to twine round the support once it has touched the support with one of its tendrils. It continues to climb in the same direction. Keep watering your plant and it should eventually produce some runner beans.

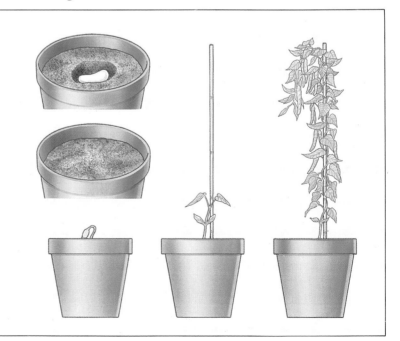

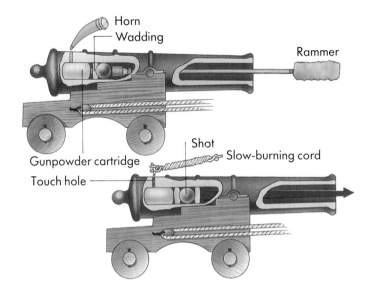

◄ *Gunpowder was needed to fire cannons on ships from the 1600s to the 1800s. A cartridge containing gunpowder was pushed into the barrel. This was followed by some wadding and a cannon ball. The cartridge was pricked and the touchhole at the breech was filled with powder. It was lit with a slow burning cord. The powder in the touch hole burnt through to the gunpowder. When this happened the gunpowder exploded and the cannon ball shot out of the cannon.*

Gunpowder

Gunpowder is a fast-burning EXPLOSIVE material that releases rapidly expanding GAS when ignited. In the confined space of a gun-barrel, this gas can give a bullet a very great ACCELERATION as it is shot out of the gun.

Gunpowder was traditionally made from saltpetre (potassium nitrate) a substance derived from plant and animal material that has decayed and oxidized, charcoal and sulphur. Gunpowder was developed by the ancient Chinese. Since the 19th century, other forms of gunpowder have been developed, not only to fire ammunition but also for use in FIREWORKS and for quarry blasting. Sodium nitrate sometimes replaces saltpetre in gunpowder used for these particular purposes. Smokeless gunpowders such as cordite include the powerful liquid explosive NITROGLYCERINE.

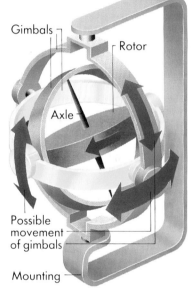

Gyrocompass

A gyrocompass is a type of COMPASS, used for direction-finding. The simplest type of compass uses a magnetized needle which swings to point at the North Pole. In fact, it points at the magnetic North Pole, which is not in the same place as the geographic or true North Pole. The gyrocompass, designed by Dr Hermann Anschutz-Kaempfe in 1905, does not rely on MAGNETISM. A GYROSCOPE is pointed at the true North Pole and starts spinning. Then, wherever the gyroscope goes, the needle turns to point to the North Pole.

▲ *A gyrocompass shows the direction of North like a magnetic compass but it does not use magnetism. Instead, it contains a spinning disc like a gyroscope. The disc is powered by an electric motor so that it spins non-stop. The axle of the disc always points in the same direction and can be set to point North. As the vessel changes direction, the mounting gimballs turn so that the rotor axle still points North.*

GYROSCOPE

▶ *Gyroscopes consist of a wheel and an axle. This gyroscope is mounted in two rings, called gimbals, and so the axis of spin is free to point in the same direction no matter how the gyroscope is held. This is used to keep instruments in one position because any force that tries to move them will be resisted by the gyroscope.*

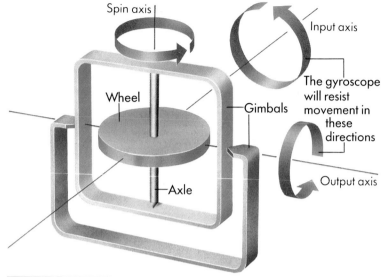

Spin axis

Input axis

Wheel

The gyroscope will resist movement in these directions

Gimbals

Axle

Output axis

▼ *When the wheel of a toy gyroscope is set spinning it can be balanced on a pencil point and will not fall as long as it spins fast enough. When the gyroscope wheel is spinning, the wheel's axle points continuously in the direction it is first set at.*

Gyroscope

A gyroscope is a disc or wheel which is spun around on its axis. Once it is set spinning, its direction of ROTATION tends to remain the same and so the direction of the spin also remains the same. The pull of GRAVITY will try to upset a gyroscope but while it is spinning it will be countered by another FORCE called PRECESSION. Precession is the tendency of spinning bodies to move at right angles to any force that tries to change its direction of rotation. This effect can be used to help with the navigation of ships and aircraft. Because the gyroscope resists changes in its direction of rotation, it can be used to indicate the direction in which the ship or aircraft is pointing compared with the direction in which the gyroscope was first set spinning.

See also GYROCOMPASS; GYROSTABILIZER.

SEE FOR YOURSELF
You can demonstrate the effect of precession, the change in direction of the spin axis as displayed by a gyroscope, with a bicycle wheel. Spin the bicycle wheel fast. Try to twist the spinning wheel by pushing down with your left hand. The wheel will move at right angles to the source of the pressure (towards the left).

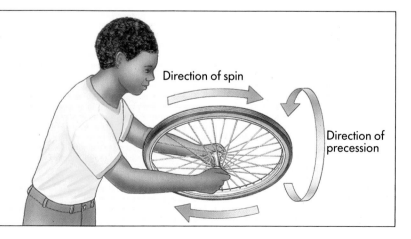

Direction of spin

Direction of precession

Animal Gyroscopes
The three fluid-filled semicircular canals are located in the ear. They are important organs for balance. When the head is moved, the fluid moves in a particular direction. The semicircular canals are set at angles to each other so that any movement affects a different combination of them. Messages are sent to the brain which help us to keep our balance. In the same way the pivoting rings of the gyroscope enable the

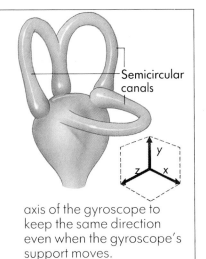

Semicircular canals

axis of the gyroscope to keep the same direction even when the gyroscope's support moves.

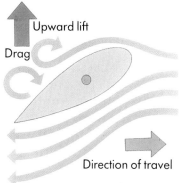

Upward lift

Drag

Direction of travel

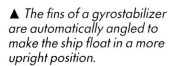

Gyrostabilizer

A gyrostabilizer is a piece of equipment designed to steady or stabilize whatever it is attached to. It relies on the tendency of a GYROSCOPE to resist any FORCE that tries to tilt it while it is spinning. Gyrostabilizers are often used to counteract the rolling motion of a ship to make the voyage more comfortable for passengers. A gyrostabilizer consists of a pair of swivelling fins, one mounted on each side of the ship, linked to a motor-driven gyroscope. If the ship starts to roll, the fins try to swivel. The gyroscope resists the motion of the fins and they in turn resist the rolling of the ship.
See also SERVOMECHANISM.

▲ *The fins of a gyrostabilizer are automatically angled to make the ship float in a more upright position.*

▼ *Gyrostabilizers are large gyroscopes that are used to stabilize a ship. A spinning gyroscope resists forces that try to change the direction of its axis. This causes the gyrostabilizer to resist the force of the waves against the ship and so reduce the rolling motion.*

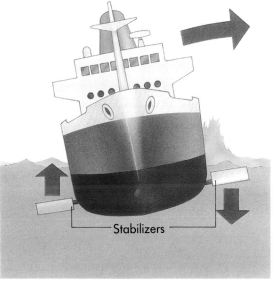

Stabilizers

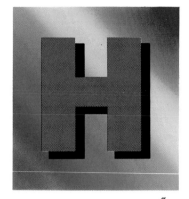

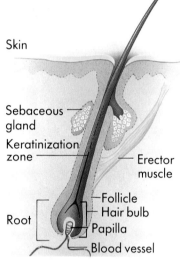

Skin

Sebaceous gland

Keratinization zone

Erector muscle

Root

Follicle
Hair bulb
Papilla
Blood vessel

▲ Hair roots are enclosed in their own bulb-like follicles, which have their own blood supply, a tiny erector muscle and a nearby sebaceous gland which produces oil.

▼ Whether hair is straight or not depends partly on the shape of the hair follicles.

Oval follicle – wavy hair

Round follicle – straight hair

Flat follicle – curly hair

Hahn, Otto *See* Nuclear physics

Hair

The presence of hair on the body is characteristic of mammals. Its function is to provide insulation to keep the body warm and to protect the SKIN. In humans, we have lost the need for insulating hair over much of our bodies, but we retain small sparse hairs over most of the body surface. Body hair in other mammals is very important. Hair can provide CAMOUFLAGE, by being coloured or marked, as in tigers and zebras. In most mammals, large hairs around the muzzle and other parts of the face are a very important sense organ. A cat relies on these hairs when moving through bushes and undergrowth to tell if it can squeeze through a gap or avoid an obstruction. The larger these whiskers are, the more important they are for that mammal.

Hair usually forms a dense coat which protects the skin from cold, and often, if it is oily provides further protection against water. Each hair grows from a small pit in the skin, called a follicle. The hair shaft is hollow and may be coloured. Tiny muscles are attached to the side of the hair, so that when they contract, the hair is raised erect increasing the thickness of the coat, keeping the mammal warmer. The same thing happens when we get 'goose pimples', and the hairs in our skin are erected.

▼ The layers of dense hair or fur of the polar bear help to protect it from the cold.

Hale, George Ellery *See* Sunspots

Half-life

The half-life of a radioactive ELEMENT is the time taken for half of it to decay, or change into a different element. It decays because it is unstable and particles from the nucleus at the centre of each ATOM escape. Some materials have half-lives of a fraction of a second. Other materials have half-lives lasting millions of years so their effects will be felt for a long time. Some elements with short half-lives can be used as tracers. If they are injected into the body or swallowed, they will show up on X-RAY pictures. This enables doctors to look for abnormalities in soft tissue that would not normally show up on an X-ray. Carbon-14, a type of carbon, is present in all living things and it can be used to discover how old things are.
See also BARIUM; CARBON DATING; RADIOISOTOPE.

▼ The element radon 222 takes approximately four days for half the original amount of atoms to decay. It has a half-life of four days. After a further four days, half of the remaining radon has decayed, and so on. As it decays the loss of an alpha particle from the radon 222 changes the radon into polonium 218.

▶ Some elements decay by losing an alpha particle, which is the same as the nucleus of a helium atom. Other elements decay by losing a beta particle, which is an electron. The table on the right shows the radioactive series that begins with uranium 238 and ends with lead. The half-life of each change is given.

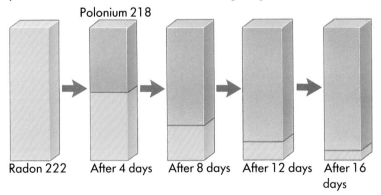

Polonium 218

Radon 222 — After 4 days — After 8 days — After 12 days — After 16 days

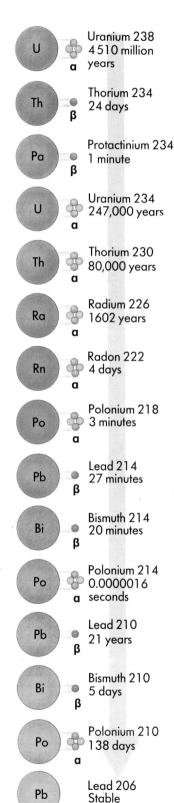

U	Uranium 238 — 4510 million years — α
Th	Thorium 234 — 24 days — β
Pa	Protactinium 234 — 1 minute — β
U	Uranium 234 — 247,000 years — α
Th	Thorium 230 — 80,000 years — α
Ra	Radium 226 — 1602 years — α
Rn	Radon 222 — 4 days — α
Po	Polonium 218 — 3 minutes — α
Pb	Lead 214 — 27 minutes — β
Bi	Bismuth 214 — 20 minutes — β
Po	Polonium 214 — 0.0000016 seconds — α
Pb	Lead 210 — 21 years — β
Bi	Bismuth 210 — 5 days — β
Po	Polonium 210 — 138 days — α
Pb	Lead 206 — Stable

Halley's Comet

Halley's is the most famous COMET of all, though it is not the largest or brightest. It takes about 76 years to orbit the SUN, and its first recorded sighting was 239 BC. After the comet has passed close to the Sun, it travels nearly to

Edmund Halley (1656–1742)
Halley was an English astronomer and physicist. He is best known for his discoveries about the orbits of comets. He calculated that the orbits of comets seen in 1531, 1607 and 1682 were very similar and from this predicted that the comet he had observed in 1682 would return in 1758. The comet appeared on Christmas Day 1758 and was named Halley's Comet in his honour.

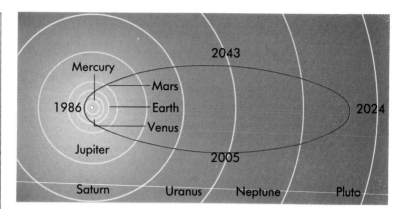

▲ *Halley's Comet last passed close to the Earth in 1986. By 2024 it will have reached the furthest point on its orbit.*

Pluto before returning. In 1705, the astronomer Edmund Halley suggested that the comet would return in 1758. It reappeared, as predicted, which was important proof that the law of GRAVITY, which explained the orbits of the Moon and planets, also worked for comets.

At its last return, in 1986, six spacecraft went close to Halley's Comet, three passing through its tail. Although its tail (of gas and dust from the rocky nucleus) could have stretched nearly halfway from the Earth to the Sun, the nucleus itself was only about 12 by 6 km!

9 **F** **19.0**	Fluorine Atomic number 9 Atomic weight 19.0
17 **Cl** **35.5**	Chlorine Atomic number 17 Atomic weight 35.5
35 **Br** **79.9**	Bromine Atomic number 35 Atomic weight 79.9
53 **I** **126.9**	Iodine Atomic number 53 Atomic weight 126.9
85 **At** **210.0**	Astatine Atomic number 85 Atomic weight 210.0

▲ *The halogens are a group of five reactive elements. Fluorine (F), chlorine (Cl), bromine (Br), iodine (I) and astatine (At).*

Halogens

Halogens are a class of five non-metallic ELEMENTS that have similar chemical characteristics and belong to Group VII of the PERIODIC TABLE. The halogen elements are fluorine, CHLORINE, bromine, IODINE and astatine. They all react with metals and with hydrogen to form COMPOUNDS called halides. Many halides are found in sea water. In their pure form, all the halogens are poisonous and will burn the skin. Fluorine is a pale yellow gas. Calcium fluoride (fluorspar) is used in refining steel and in making aluminium. Very small amounts of fluorides are added to drinking water to prevent tooth decay. Bromine is a reddish-brown, volatile liquid used mainly in making dyes, medicines and chemicals for fighting fires. Light-sensitive silver bromide, like silver iodide, is used in the photographic industry. Astatine, the heaviest of the halogens, is a radioactive element with no stable ISO-TOPES. It is used in medicine as a tracer. In a halogen lamp, adding a little iodine to the tungsten filament produces a whiter light than a conventional light bulb. The most important halogen is chlorine.

Hard water

Water which does not produce a good lather with soap is known as hard water. Consequently, water which does produce a good lather is called soft water. The hardness is caused by COMPOUNDS dissolved in the water.

When water passes through ROCKS and SOILS, some of the compounds are dissolved into the water. There are two kinds of hardness: temporary and permanent. Temporary hardness may be removed by boiling the water. It is caused by calcium hydrogencarbonate dissolved in the water when the water has passed through limestones such as chalk. When boiled, the soluble hydrogencarbonates change to insoluble calcium carbonates producing a scum which forms the 'fur' found in kettles in hard-water areas.

Permanent hardness can be removed by systems called 'ion exchange' water softeners, such as Permutit.

Elements causing hard water include the chlorides, carbonates and sulphates of metals such as sodium, calcium, magnesium and iron. Permanent hardness cannot be removed by boiling the water. It is caused by calcium sulphate and other salts dissolved in the water and, in areas where the water is permanently hard, it is still difficult to get a lather from soap even after the water has been boiled.

◄ *This effect can be seen on the walls of caves in hard-water areas. Water containing calcium carbonate seeps into the caves, and builds up into a solid mineral formation.*

Hardness

The hardness of a SOLID, such as a METAL or MINERAL is measured by its ability to resist being scratched or indented. Hardness depends on the size of its ATOMS, the strength of their BONDS and the way they are packed. The closely-packed structure and small size of the atoms in DIAMOND contribute to its hardness, however, in soft graphite, the atoms are loosely bonded.

Hard materials wear away softer ones so it is necessary to know the relative hardness of materials such as ABRASIVES. This is particularly important when making and using tools. The hardness of minerals is usually measured on a scale called the Mohs' scale.

SEE FOR YOURSELF
Make a chart of the hardness of different pencils. Soft pencils are usually labelled with a B. They make thick black lines that are easily smudged. Hard pencils, labelled with an H, make a fine line. Very hard pencils may scratch the surface of the paper. You can estimate the hardness of other things by seeing if a pencil will scratch it.

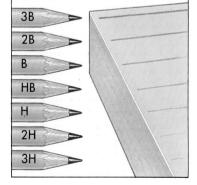

Mohs' Scale of Hardness

In 1822 the German mineralogist Friedrich Mohs made a list of 10 common minerals from which hardness could be measured. The mineral labelled 1 is the softest and the mineral labelled 10 the hardest. Because mineral 10 is hardest it can therefore scratch mineral 9, mineral 9 can scratch mineral 8 and so on down the scale. Talc, the softest mineral on Moh's scale, can be scratched with a finger nail. The minerals are:
diamond **10**, corundum **9**, topaz **8**, quartz **7**, orthoclase **6**, apatite **5**, fluorite **4**, calcite **3**, gypsum **2** and talc **1**.

1. Talc
2. Gypsum
3. Calcite
4. Fluorite
5. Apatite
6. Orthoclase
7. Quartz
8. Topaz
9. Corundum
10. Diamond

A fingernail has a hardness of about 2½

A copper coin has a hardness of about 3½

Minerals of 6 or more can scratch glass

A penknife has a hardness of 5½ and can scratch apatite but not orthoclase

A special steel file can scratch quartz

The first electronic computer, built in 1945, weighed 30 tonnes and filled a large hall of 140 square metres; it contained more than 18,000 valves. However, it was no more powerful than a small home computer of today. The development of the transistor and then the microchip mean that much less hardware is needed for today's computers. Modern computers are compact and powerful; most will fit on a desktop.

Hardware

Hardware is the physical part of an ELECTRONIC system, the electronic components and CIRCUITS that enable the system to function. 'Hardware' is most frequently used to describe one of the two basic parts of a COMPUTER system, the other part being the computer programs, or SOFTWARE, that control the hardware. Each is useless without the other. The hardware of a computer system is its keyboard, screen, disk drives and electronic circuits. Hardware and software are also commonly used terms in connection with TELEVISION and video. The hardware in

▶ A mainframe computer is a large powerful piece of hardware. This high-speed computer has a large storage capacity, to which one or more work stations have access.

308

the home consists of VIDEO RECORDERS and television sets. They are useless without the software, such as television programmes and films. The magnetic disks and tapes for recording and storing computer programs are also described as software.

Harmonics

Harmonics are the different FREQUENCIES at which something can vibrate. For example, a string stretched between two supports can vibrate so that different numbers of WAVELENGTHS of the wave can fit along the string. The wave with the longest wavelength is called the fun-

The quality of sound made by a musical instrument, the timbre, depends on a number of factors. The most important of these is the relative intensity of the harmonics, or overtones, produced. A note made by a violin has a full and vibrant sound because it is rich in overtones. A note made by a flute is almost a pure tone because it is produced by a vibration that has no overtones.

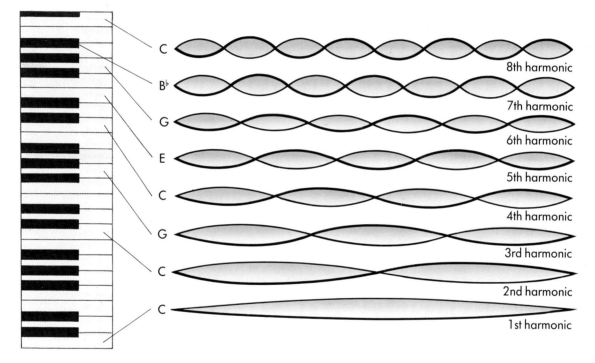

C — 8th harmonic
B♭ — 7th harmonic
G — 6th harmonic
E — 5th harmonic
C — 4th harmonic
G — 3rd harmonic
C — 2nd harmonic
C — 1st harmonic

damental; the other vibrations have wavelengths one half, one third, one quarter and so on times the fundamental wavelength and frequencies two, three, four and so on times the fundamental frequency. This series of frequencies is known as the harmonic series. There are similar series for the SOUND waves in pipes.

A musical note corresponds to a sound wave of a particular frequency; the different sounds of different-shaped MUSICAL INSTRUMENTS come from the different mixtures of harmonics of the fundamental notes.

▲ *A series of harmonics sound when a piano string vibrates. The position of the notes on the piano keyboard which give these harmonics are shown above. When these keys shown are pressed down without sounding them and the bottom key, C, is struck firmly, the harmonics will resonate.*

Harvey, William *See* Circulation

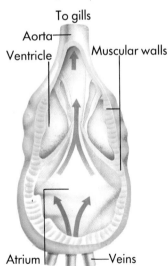

To gills

Aorta
Ventricle — Muscular walls

Atrium — Veins

▲ *In some vertebrate animals such as most reptiles, amphibians and fish, the heart is not a double-pump structure.*

▶ *The human heart is really two pumps side by side. The right side (left side of diagram) pumps oxygen-poor blood to the lungs. The left side pumps oxygen-rich blood to the body's cells.*

310

Hawking, Stephen *See* Black hole

Hearing *See* Ear

Heart

The heart is a muscular organ which pumps BLOOD around the body through arteries, capillaries and veins as it contracts rhythmically. In mammals, birds and crocodiles the blood is passed through a double CIRCULATION. The heart pumps blood from the right side of the heart to the LUNGS, then blood carrying OXYGEN returns to the left side of the heart to be pumped around the rest of the body. The heart is actually a pair of pumps, on each side of which the upper chamber or atrium collects in-coming blood, then passes it through a one-way valve into the muscular ventricle beneath. This ventricle then contracts strongly and propels blood out of the heart and away to the lungs or the rest of the body. The human heart is mostly MUSCLE, and contracts or pumps about 70 times each minute. Contractions are controlled by a timing mechanism, which keeps the heart beating evenly. The speed of pumping can be increased by HORMONES and NERVE impulses when extra exertion means that more oxygen is needed in the tissues.

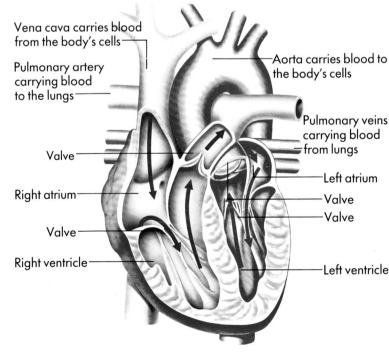

Vena cava carries blood from the body's cells

Pulmonary artery carrying blood to the lungs

Valve

Right atrium

Valve

Right ventricle

Aorta carries blood to the body's cells

Pulmonary veins carrying blood from lungs

Left atrium

Valve

Valve

Left ventricle

Heat

Heat is produced by the conversion of other forms of ENERGY. Heat is formed from kinetic energy by FRICTION. Electrical energy is converted into heat by an electric fire and during cooking. The food we eat is used to heat our bodies. *See* pages 312 and 313.

Heat exchanger

A heat exchanger is used to transfer HEAT from a hot object or space, to a cooler object or space. Heat exchangers are widely used for cooling MACHINES. Most vehicle ENGINES are cooled by circulating water around the engine. This is warmed by the hot engine and pumped to a radiator. Air rushing past the radiator cools the hot water inside. A hot liquid can be cooled by pumping it through a pipe surrounded by cold water. The heat transfers to the water. Spacecraft are cooled by emitting INFRARED RADIATION into space from radiators.

Heat pump

A heat pump is used to transfer HEAT from a cooler object or space, to a warmer one. Heat cannot flow in this direction without ENERGY because it normally flows from hot to cold. Refrigerators use heat pumps. A FLUID called a refrigerant is allowed to expand and change into a VAPOUR in the fridge's freezing compartment. It takes the energy it needs for this from the freezer, cooling it in the process. The vapour is then compressed and passed through a condenser where it changes back to a liquid, giving out the energy from the freezer as heat. The same principle is used in AIR CONDITIONING systems.

▲ As cooled blood from the foot of an Arctic bird travels up its leg it comes into close contact with warm blood in the artery. The bird's foot acts as a heat exchanger.

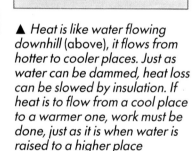

▲ Heat is like water flowing downhill (above), it flows from hotter to cooler places. Just as water can be dammed, heat loss can be slowed by insulation. If heat is to flow from a cool place to a warmer one, work must be done, just as it is when water is raised to a higher place (bottom).

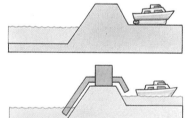

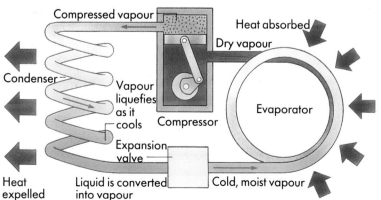

◀ A household refrigerator is a type of heat pump. It absorbs heat from the food inside it by the evaporator. The dry vapour is then compressed and as it cools it gives out heat energy as it becomes liquid. The heat is then passed into the outside air.

HEAT

Heat is a form of energy. Heat is stored in the form of motions and vibrations of the atoms which make up materials; the amount of vibration determines the temperature of the material. Larger objects contain more heat energy than smaller objects at the same temperature.

Heat travels from hotter bodies to colder ones, so it tends to even out differences in temperature. This is a consequence of the second law of thermodynamics which states that heat cannot be transferred from a colder to a hotter body without the addition of energy. There are three main ways in which heat can travel; by electromagnetic radiation; by conduction through a material of any sort; and by convection, which involves the circulation of a liquid or a gas which carries heat with it.

The molecules of an object are affected by heat energy. The most obvious effect of the loss or gain of heat energy is a change of state. A solid, for example, may melt, or a liquid may freeze, or it may boil and vaporize. Less obvious is the expansion or contraction of a material. Almost all substances expand when heated and contract when cooled because of the increased or decreased energy in the molecules.

Our bodies have to be maintained at a certain temperature which is high enough so that molecules are moving around quickly enough for chemical reactions to take place, but not so quickly that the molecules are changed.

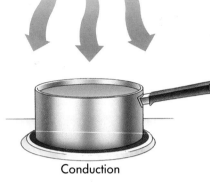

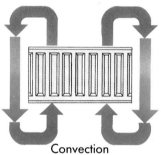

▲ Heat travels from the Sun by radiation in a stream of waves. When heat is conducted through the metal of a cooking pot, the metal molecules vibrate back and forth passing heat energy from one molecule to the next. When heat is carried through a fluid such as air, molecules in the air move, taking heat with them.

◀ Heat is generated in furnaces in which metals are produced. These two carbon electrodes are very hot because large amounts of electricity flow through them.

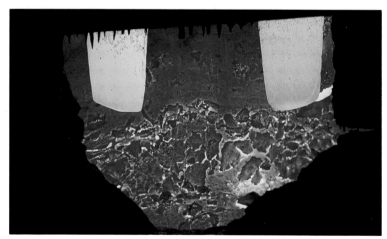

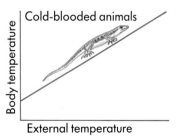

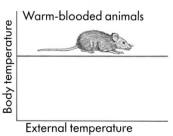

◀ In many animals such as lizards, the body temperature fluctuates with the temperature of the surroundings. They are called cold-blooded animals though their temperature can rise much higher than that of warm-blooded animals, such as mammals. Warm-blooded animals maintain their body at a stable temperature despite changes in the external temperature.

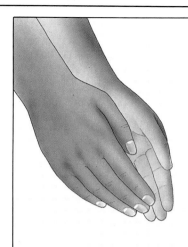

SEE FOR YOURSELF
Rub your hands together. You will find that they get warm. The heat energy comes from friction. The energy given off by a light bulb is 95 percent heat. You can feel this by holding your hands about 30 cm away from a naked light bulb. Do this for just a short time. Compare the intensity of the heat given off by a 25, 40 and 60 watt bulb. **Do not touch the bulbs because they could be very hot.**

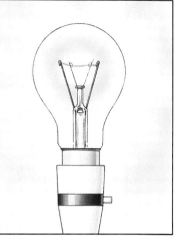

Latent Heat

Heat makes liquids boil and solids melt. When heat is added to a solid, such as ice, its temperature is raised to melting point. The temperature stops rising and remains constant until all the ice has melted, then it will rise again.

▶ *The human body generates energy and heat from carbohydrates in food. Heat is produced as a waste product by muscles when they have been doing work, for example, running. The body sweats to cool down.*

Joules are the main unit used to measure heat in the international SI units systems. The **calorie** has also been used as a unit. One calorie is equal to 4.1855 joules. One calorie is the amount of heat needed to raise the temperature of 1 gram of water through 1°C. Calories as well as joules are used to measure the energy content of foods, but because this energy can be quite large, the usual unit is the kilojoule (kJ) equal to 1000 joules or kilocalories, which are often just referred to as calories.

SEE FOR YOURSELF
You need 2 large plastic beakers. Pour a cup of vinegar into each of the beakers. Heat the vinegar in one of the beakers by standing it in very hot water for a few minutes. Add a tablespoon of bicarbonate of soda (sodium hydrogencarbonate) to each beaker. Both solutions start to foam as carbon dioxide gas is produced. The cold solution foams steadily, whereas the heated solution foams violently for a short while and then goes flat. This is because the heat speeds up the reaction between the vinegar and the bicarbonate of soda.

See also CONDUCTION, HEAT; CONVECTION; ELECTROMAGNETIC RADIATION; ENERGY; INSULATION, THERMAL; RADIATION; TEMPERATURE.

▲ *Parts of the Space Shuttle are exposed to temperatures of over 1500°C during re-entry to the Earth's atmosphere. Heat resistant tiles made of carbon and silicon are used to insulate the shuttle.*

▼ *The nose of the Space Shuttle being tested for heat resistance in a furnace.*

▶ *The Romans built underfloor heating systems, known as hypocausts, to heat their buildings. Air was heated by a furnace. It would then travel through a series of columns and archways under the floor and through hollow walls. The heat would then rise up to warm the rooms above it.*

Heat shield

A heat shield is a layer of heat-resistant material applied to part of a rocket or spacecraft to protect it from high TEMPERATURES. In particular, it protects the spacecraft from the intense HEAT it experiences when it re-enters the Earth's ATMOSPHERE from space. The heat is a result of FRICTION between the air and the vehicle. Originally, heat shields were made from materials that burned very slowly and could only be used once. The US space shuttle uses a new type of heat shield that can be used over and over again like the spacecraft itself.

Heating systems

Heating systems are used to warm the spaces that people live, work and travel in. They differ in detail but they all operate on the same principles. All heating systems generate the ENERGY needed to warm living spaces by

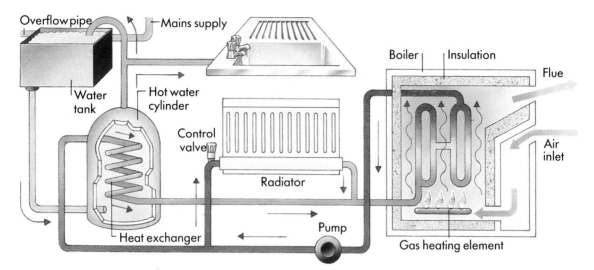

BURNING a FUEL such as oil, gas or coal. Electric systems obtain their energy from a power station which in turn generates energy by burning a fuel. Solar heating systems use energy collected from the SUN, where it was also generated by burning a fuel, hydrogen. Wherever the energy comes from, it is usually used to heat water and this is then pumped around flattened hollow metal panels called radiators. Their large surface area allows the maximum heat exchange between the hot water and the surrounding air. The water in the radiators is returned to a boiler, where it is heated and pumped around the radiators again. This is commonly known as central heating. Shops and offices frequently use a system called AIR CONDITIONING, where the TEMPERATURE and HUMIDITY of the air circulating through them is controlled by HEAT EXCHANGERS and humidifiers.

▲ In a hot-water heating system, fuel is burned in a boiler, which heats the water in the central heating system. The same water is pumped round the system, called a closed system, heating up and cooling down. Hot water is pumped along one set of pipes which heat the water in the tank that supplies hot water. Water pumped through another set of pipes heats the radiators.

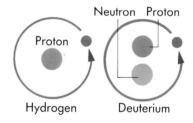

Heavy water

Heavy water is a form of water in which the HYDROGEN atoms are replaced by atoms of deuterium; it is also known as deuterium oxide. Deuterium is an ISOTOPE of hydrogen and has an ATOMIC WEIGHT double that of ordinary hydrogen. Ordinary natural water contains a minute amount of deuterium, one atom of deuterium to 6760 atoms of hydrogen. Heavy water is usually obtained by fractional DISTILLATION. Its chief use is as the substance that limits the energy of the neutrons produced during a reaction in a NUCLEAR REACTOR.

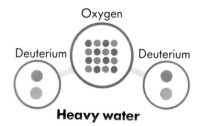

Heavy water

▲ A hydrogen atom has a single proton as its nucleus. Deuterium, or heavy hydrogen, has a proton and a neutron. Heavy water is a compound of deuterium and oxygen.

Helicopter *See* Flight

▲ *Multicoloured helium-filled balloons rise to high altitudes because helium is lighter than air.*

▶ *The equator divides the Earth into the Northern (left) and the Southern (right) hemispheres. The word hemisphere comes from the Greek word* Hemisphairion *meaning half a sphere.*

Between two-thirds and three-quarters of the Earth's surface is covered with water and, of this, by far the greater amount is to be found in the Southern Hemisphere. If you were to look from space from a point directly above the South Pole, you would see that, apart from the southern tips of the northern continents, the only significant land mass is the continent of Antarctica.

Helium

Helium is an unreactive NOBLE GAS with no colour, taste or smell. It is second only to hydrogen in lightness. Helium is formed in STARS such as the SUN as hydrogen nuclei are forced together by NUCLEAR FUSION. It is named after *helios*, the Greek for Sun. There is very little helium on Earth. The air contains five parts per million of it and it exists in certain rocks. Most of the world's helium comes from the United States, where it is found with NATURAL GAS. Helium becomes liquid at about −268.9°C (about 4°C above absolute zero) and only becomes solid under pressure, so it is used as a refrigerant and in cold-temperature physics research. Liquid helium expands rather than contracts on cooling, and when it only partly fills a container, it will creep up the sides and spill over the rim.

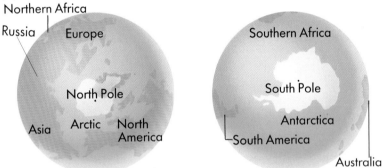

Hemisphere

A hemisphere is one half of the EARTH's globe. The two halves of the globe most usually referred to are the Northern Hemisphere, covering the area North of the equator, and the Southern Hemisphere, the area South of the equator. It is also possible to divide the Earth from the North to the South Poles along 0° and 180° lines of LONGITUDE, giving Eastern and Western Hemispheres.

The Earth orbits the SUN and spins on its own axis at an angle to the plane of the Earth's orbit. Consequently, the Northern Hemisphere is tilted towards the Sun and experiences summer between March and September when it is winter in the Southern Hemisphere.

Hemophilia (Haemophilia) *See* Genetics

Herbicide *See* Pesticide